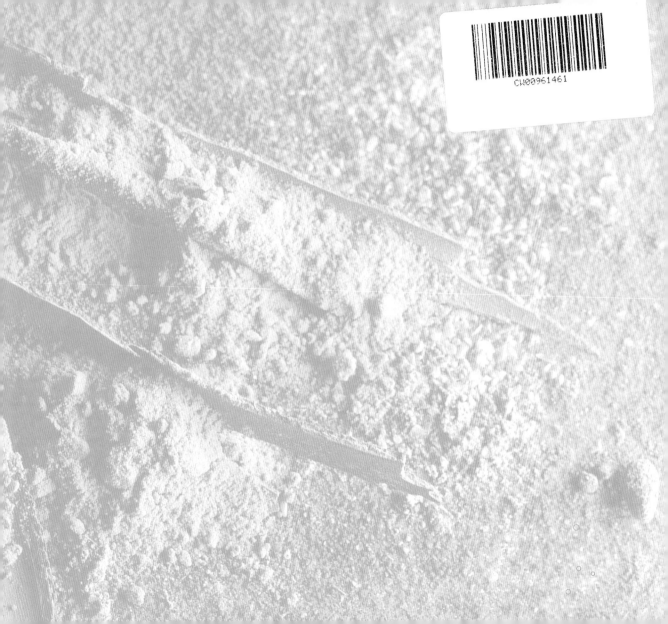

Book of Spices

Marie-Françoise Valéry

Book of Spices

Photographs by Sophie Boussahba
Drawings by Florine Asch

HACHETTE
Illustrated

For hundreds of years spices were regarded as a highly precious commodity, and people were prepared to risk their lives to obtain them, making long and perilous journeys through deserts and across the high seas. This 14th-century illustration shows a spice merchant in his shop.

Contents

Introduction

Spices are aromatic vegetable substances that consist of the seeds, bark, flowers, fruit or berries of plants. Their flavours range from sweet to fiery, and today they are used primarily to flavour food. Many spices also have medicinal properties, and some are even credited with having aphrodisiac powers. In the past, spices were used to flavour bland dishes, or to mask the rancid or bitter taste of food that could not be kept fresh over long periods of time.

Spices were once so highly prized that some, such as cinnamon, were almost worth their weight in gold. It was the European quest for spices that took Marco Polo to the Far East and drove Christopher Columbus to seek a swifter sea route to India. As ships returned laden with cloves, pepper, nutmeg and ginger, the spice trade also brought cities such as Venice, Lisbon and Rotterdam fabulous wealth.

With the advent of efficient refrigeration and other modern methods of conserving food, spices were no longer so highly prized and the full panoply of their exotic flavours, which once conjured up long sea journeys to distant lands, was gradually forgotten. However, spices are enjoying a resurgence in Western cuisine; many leading chefs now skilfully use their unique flavours in fish and meat dishes as well as in desserts.

Eastern spices

*A*lthough spices come from all over the world, they are most closely associated with the East. A large number of spices come from plants indigenous to India, China, Indonesia and Japan. The lure of Eastern spices drew countless explorers and navigators on journeys to the other side of the world. Later, to meet European demand, extensive plantations were established in countries where spices once grew wild.

Star anise

The flavour of this distinctively star-shaped spice is similar to that of aniseed, although it is stronger and sharper, with a hint of liquorice.

FRUIT OF AN ANCIENT TREE

Star anise is the dried fruit of a small evergreen tree indigenous to China. This tree, *Illicium verum*, grows very slowly, and does not start to bear fruit until six years after germination. After about 15 years, it produces an abundant crop and between its 25th and 100th year a tree can produce over 40 kg (88 lb) fruit each year.

The tree has lustrous leaves similar to that of the magnolia, and a yellow flower. The flower matures into a fruit whose pods, or carpels, form a star shape. Each pod contains a small round seed, which is hard, brown and shiny.

PODS AND SEEDS

Just before they are fully ripe the pods are harvested and laid out to dry in the sun. Both the pods and the seeds are used as a spice, either separately or together, and they are added to dishes whole, crushed or ground. The pods have a stronger flavour than the seeds.

The carpels of star anise contain small round seeds. Both the carpels and the seeds are used in cooking, either whole or in powdered form.

Opposite page:
Star anise, peppercorns, chillies and sweet peppers. A selection of spices and peppers used in Guyanese cuisine, in which star anise predominates.

GINGERBREAD AND CHINESE CUISINE

Star anise is extensively used in Chinese cookery, particularly to impart a sweet and spicy flavour. Star anise is also an ingredient of Chinese five-spice powder, whose other components are pepper, cinnamon, fennel and cloves.

Also used in Indian cuisine, star anise is one of the constituents of curry powder. In all Eastern cookery, it enhances sweet and savoury dishes and is readily added to meat, fish and vegetable dishes. In Western cookery it is more often used with vegetables and in cakes, and is also used to flavour gingerbread, ice cream, herbal teas and mulled wine.

Like all spices, star anise gives the most intense flavour when it is freshly crushed or ground immediately before use, either as part of a recipe's ingredients or sprinkled straight on to a dish just before serving.

Salmon with star anise and fresh rosemary

Serves 6

*6 pieces of salmon,
150 g (5 oz) each
2 tablespoons of flour
30 g (1 oz) of butter
the juice of 1 lemon
1 sprig of rosemary, chopped
6 star anise*

Wash the salmon pieces, pat them dry and coat in flour. Melt the butter in a pan and, over a medium heat, cook the salmon on both sides for a total of 5 minutes.

Arrange the salmon pieces in a warmed dish. Pour over the lemon juice and garnish with the rosemary and the star anise.

Alternatively, the salmon can be poached in a flavoured stock. Tie a few star anise, with some fresh thyme and fresh rosemary, in muslin. Add this to the water in which the salmon is poached.

Cinnamon

Cinnamon has been used as a spice since ancient times, and it is mentioned several times in the Bible. For example, 'sweet cinnamon' is one of the principal spices that made up an anointing oil prepared by Moses.

Cinnamon sticks are made from the bark of the cinnamon tree. Cut into strips, the bark rolls up into quills as it dries.

FRAGRANT BARK

Cinnamon, the aromatic inner bark of the cinnamon tree, is a spice that from ancient times has been the object of extensive trade networks. Since at least 4000 BC the Arabs, followed by the Greeks and then the Romans, launched expeditions as far as the East Indies to obtain this highly prized spice, which was valued for its culinary uses. In the 16th century control of the cinnamon trade passed to the Portuguese, who were established in Sri Lanka, where the cinnamon tree originated. This monopoly later passed to the Dutch, and then to the British. In the 19th century, the French seafarer Pierre Poivre (see page 29) challenged this monopoly when he established a cinnamon plantation in Mauritius, which was then known as the Île de France.

A TREE OF THE LAUREL FAMILY

The cinnamon tree, *Cinnamomum zeylanicum*, is indigenous to Sri Lanka, and this island still provides the most fragrant cinnamon in the world. In its natural state the tree grows to a height of about 10 metres (33 feet). Under cultivation, cinnamon trees are kept to the size of a shrub, being pruned in such a way that they produce many branches. The cinnamon tree, which belongs to the laurel family, is an evergreen with tough, lustrous leaves that are oval and veined. It has white flowers and small black berries. The inner bark is the only part of the tree that is used to produce the spice known as cinnamon. The tree thrives in sandy soil in a

Canelle.

Canelle Sauvage.

Canelle Blanche.

Canelle Girofflée.

hot and humid climate, and needs full exposure to the sun for the bark to develop its full aroma.

A SWEET AND INTENSE FLAVOUR

During the Middle Ages, cinnamon was used mostly to flavour meat and sauces. This is also its primary use in Eastern countries, where cinnamon is used in many savoury dishes, including stews, and with game and vegetables. In Western cuisine, cinnamon is more generally used in sweet dishes, to add flavour to creams, apple pies, fruit compote and fruit salad, and it is also sprinkled on buttered toast.

There are several different varieties of cinnamon tree, including cassia, or bastard cinnamon, whose bark is used as a substitute for true cinnamon. It is only the bark of *Cinnamomum zeylanicum*, which is indigenous to Sri Lanka, that produces genuine cinnamon sticks.

Cinnamon bark is also used to make small cylindrical boxes.

Harvesting cinnamon bark

Cinnamon trees are pruned twice a year, during the spring and autumn rainy seasons. This not only stimulates the growth of new shoots but also keeps the tree to the size of a shrub, which makes it easier for cultivators to harvest the bark.

When the bark is harvested, shoots of three or four years' growth are cut and stripped of their leaves. Two incisions are made with a knife: one around the thickness of the shoot and the other vertically along its length. The bark can then come away quite easily, in the shape of a small rectangle. The bark is laid out in the sun and as it dries it curls up into quills. The quills are then packed one inside the other and neatly trimmed, to form cinnamon sticks.

Cardamom

Cardamom may be named after the Cardamom Hills, in southern India, where it grows in the forests that line the Malabar coast. Cardamom is indigenous to this region, but it is also grown in Cambodia and Sri Lanka.

White cardamom seeds in a mortar and, right, green cardamom, the most strongly flavoured variety.

THE SPICE PLANT WITH IRIS-LIKE FLOWERS

Like vanilla and saffron, cardamom is one of the most expensive of all spices. This is because the plant that it comes from, *Elettaria cardamomum*, flowers only after two or three years of careful nurturing and because harvesting its seeds is a time-consuming and painstaking process. The cardamom is a perennial plant similar to ginger and turmeric. Like the iris, it has a rhizome, or thick horizontal stem, that puts out vertical shoots. In shape the plant is similar to bamboo, and it can grow to a height of 4 metres (13 feet) or more. The shoots are covered with long, pointed leaves, and the flowers are white with blue throats, resembling iris flowers.

PAINSTAKING HARVEST

Cardamom thrives in a moist, tropical climate. It grows in forested areas, particularly along the banks of streams and rivers. New plants can be grown by splitting the rhizome. Cardamom flowers in the first half of the year and its fruits, small pods containing seeds, are gathered in the second half, while they are still quite green and have the strongest flavour. The pods are delicately picked or clipped from the plant, great care being taken not to damage them. They are then laid out in the sun to dry.

LEMON AND EUCALYPTUS FLAVOURS

Cardamom seed pods are sold in three grades: green, white and brown. Green cardamoms contain the most strongly flavoured seeds. The white ones have been blanched to give them a more attractive colour but they are often of an inferior quality. Brown cardamoms have a much less pungent flavour.

The best way to buy cardamom is in the form of pods rather than as husked seeds or as cardamom powder, which quickly loses its flavour. The seeds can be used whole, crushed or ground and they release their fullest flavour if they are husked just before use. Placed in a closed container, in a cool, dry place, cardamom pods keep well for relatively long periods of time.

With its pungent lemon and eucalyptus aroma, cardamom is used in many Indian dishes, particularly curries. In North Africa, cardamom is used to flavour coffee, and the seeds are also chewed to sweeten the breath. In the West, cardamom is used to flavour tea, and is also added to creams, ice cream, fruit compote and fruit pies. It can also be used to flavour baked pears and baked apples or fruit salads.

Spiced teas are very popular in Japan. Trays laid out for the Japanese tea ceremony are often decorated, as here, with a bundle of bamboo tea, cinnamon sticks and cardamom pods.

Spiced teas

In China, Sri Lanka, the East Indies and other Eastern regions spiced tea is a very popular drink. By happy coincidence these areas produce not only the most renowned teas but also the most aromatic spices. Although, for purists, the finest teas, in all their varieties, are best enjoyed with no additional flavouring, tea blended with certain dried flowers, fruit, herbs or spices makes a delectable drink. While some teas are sold ready-mixed with ginger, cardamom or cinnamon, deliciously spiced teas or herbal infusions can be prepared at home by adding a stick of cinnamon, a few grains of aniseed, some cardamom seeds or a few cloves to the pot.

The spice trade

It could almost be said that the quest for spices has altered the course of history. The story of the spice trade is itself peopled by great travellers and seafarers, who risked their lives to reach the most distant corners of the world. They returned with cargoes of spices, whose exotic aromas can transform the blandest dish into a feast of subtle flavours.

An Arab monopoly

Knowledge of spices, and of their multifarious uses, goes back to very ancient times. The trade in these vegetable substances, which were used to enhance the flavour of food and prized for their medicinal uses, were the monopoly of the Arabs, who journeyed to the Far East to obtain them. Spices were in equally high demand among the ancient Greeks and Romans, who embarked on perilous sea voyages to the East Indies to secure supplies. They also established a land route to China, returning not only with spices but also with precious stones and silks.

The spice trade remained under Arab control through the Middle Ages. Caravans brought spices to market in Alexandria, where they were purchased by Venetian merchants who then sold them on to European distributors for exorbitant prices. At this time, these rare and precious commodities were destined only for the kitchens and apothecaries of monasteries and royal palaces. Contemporary writings record that, during the Middle Ages, monks were using pepper, cinnamon, cloves, cumin, coriander, cardamom and ginger.

Above:
The Arkesilas Dish, which dates from the 6th century BC, is painted with a scene illustrating the trade in silphium, one of the rarest spices in the ancient world. Over time, silphium fell out of use and today we do not even know which plant it came from.

A 16th-century depiction of a caravan, with spice merchants following the overland trade route to Asia.

Asia and its spices

Marco Polo wrote enthralling accounts of his travels in India and Asia. Published in the 13th century, they fired the enthusiasm of generations of travellers. Marco Polo was not, however, the pioneer of the European overland spice routes. His father, Niccolo, and his uncle, Matteo, both wealthy Venetian merchants, had followed the route to China some twenty years earlier. But Marco Polo's accounts whetted the European appetite for spices, and countries with large fleets at their disposal established a trade that was to continue for several hundred years.

The race for spices

At the end of the 15th century the Portuguese joined in the race to obtain spices. In 1497 Vasco da Gama sailed from Lisbon with four caravels under his command. Rounding the Cape of Good Hope, he headed east towards India and reached the Malabar Coast. Further expeditions followed. The Portuguese took control of the Moluccas (or Spice Islands), in the Malay Archipelago,

and sailed on to Sri Lanka, from where their ships returned laden with spices. In the same period, the Genoan navigator Christopher Columbus set sail across the Atlantic, hoping to discover a new route to India and its spices. He reached the Americas – Cuba, the Bahamas and Haiti – but it was only from his fourth voyage, in 1502, that he returned with sweet peppers and vanilla.

Portrait of Vasco da Gama (1469–1524), the Portuguese navigator who in 1497 discovered the sea route to the Indies. This gave Portugal control of the European spice trade, which it maintained for several centuries.

Dutch supremacy

In the mid-18th century the Dutch supplanted the Portuguese, who until then had controlled the European spice trade. However, competition was by now fierce, as several other European countries had joined in this profitable trade. France, Britain, Sweden, Denmark, Austria and Prussia also launched seafaring expeditions, although none was entirely successful.

New plantations

In the 18th century, the Frenchman Pierre Poivre arrived on the Molucca Islands. Having braved the dangers of the sea voyage, he snatched spice-tree saplings from under the noses of the Dutch. He then sailed for the Île de France and the Île Bourbon, French possessions now known as the islands of Réunion and Mauritius, where he established clove, cinnamon and nutmeg plantations.

Britain, ruler of the seas

By the 19th century spices were no longer such a rare commodity. Now less expensive, they were also less highly prized. Plantations multiplied and, as sea voyages had become both safer and less costly, the shipment of spices was also easier. However, when India became part of the British Empire, the international spice trade passed to British control. Today, although London, Hamburg, Rotterdam and New York are still major centres of the spice market, spices are now universally accessible.

Above: The market in Goa in the 16th century, one of the focal points of the international spice trade.

Below: Amsterdam in 1752, during the time when the Dutch exerted exclusive control over maritime spice routes.

Cloves

The word clove *is derived from* clou, *the French term for nail. This is because cloves are remarkably similar in shape to the type of nail once used in carpentry. Cloves have a distinctive sweet, pungent and rather heady flavour. They have a multitude of uses and were once among the most highly prized of spices. It was the trade in cloves that drove the greatest land and sea journeys during the Age of Discovery.*

Indonesian bamboo spice box, an ideal receptacle for cloves.

THE BEWITCHING DOORNAIL

Cloves are the dried flower buds of a tropical variety of myrtle. Consisting of a spherical bud on a short stem, their shape is almost identical to that of a doornail, a type of nail once used in carpentry, particularly in making doors.

The clove tree, *Eugenia caryophyllus*, is probably native to the Molucca Islands, where it thrives along coastlines. Moluccan clove production was firmly in the hands of the Portuguese until 1605, when the Dutch wrested control of it, establishing other plantations of clove trees on the island of Amboina and turning the clove trade into a highly profitable monopoly. However, in the 18th century, the French seafarer Pierre Poivre successfully established a clove plantation on Mauritius and Réunion. Later he established other clove plantations throughout the West Indies and in Zanzibar and Madagascar. These are still major producers of cloves today.

GROWING AND HARVESTING

The clove tree is a magnificent evergreen that grows to a height of up to 10 metres (33 feet). It thrives in a hot and humid climate and it is planted in rows in the tropical countries where it is cultivated. The tree is productive from its sixth year and continues to flower until it is over 70 years old. It produces yellow blooms but these are picked when they are still buds. They are laid out on sheets in the sun, and as they dry they turn brown and take on their familiar shape, also developing their pungent flavour and aroma.

Giroffle Royal

Geroffle

MEDICINAL AND CULINARY USES

Having medicinal as well as culinary uses, cloves are among the most useful of all spices. A potent antiseptic, cloves disinfect wounds and assist healing, and were once widely used to treat dental abscesses as well as ulcers and digestive problems. Cloves also sweeten the breath; the Chinese, to whom the virtues of this spice were known since ancient times, still chew on cloves today.

Used in cooking, cloves impart their sweet and pungent aroma to all kinds of food, from desserts to savoury dishes. Cloves can also be used in sauces, in spiced bread and in cakes, and can be added to certain drinks, particularly fruit juices, cocktails and mulled wine. An onion pierced with cloves enhances the flavour of meat or vegetable stock.

Cloves also make excellent air fresheners. They can be added to pot-pourri or to fragrant sachets for perfuming linen and they are an essential component of pomanders.

Cloves are the dried flower bud of the clove tree. The buds are harvested just as they start to turn pink.

Pomanders

Pomanders are traditional Christmas gifts. They have an exquisite scent and are quick and easy to make at home. They can be made either with lemons or oranges, although using an orange will result in a more perfectly spherical pomander. Take a plump, round orange and, with a knitting needle, pierce the skin evenly all over. Press a clove into each hole so that only the head of the clove is visible and the surface of the orange is densely covered. The pomander should then be left to dry for about a month. Then pierce it right the way through so that you can pass a thin cord or ribbon through it. Hang the pomander from a door handle, a piece of furniture or over a mantelpiece. Its scent will perfume the air for several months.

Turmeric

Widely used in Indian cuisine, turmeric is both a spice and a food colourant. The plant has an orange rhizome which, when it is ground, produces a golden yellow powder. It is this that gives curry dishes their rich colour.

THE GOLDEN SPICE

Turmeric comes from *Curcuma longa*, a perennial plant that is native to South and South-East Asia. Because of its colouring properties, it is also known as Indian saffron and in India it is used to dye textiles a deep, rich yellow.

Above:
A turmeric plant in bloom. The flower is similar to that of the European lily or arum lily.

Taken straight from the ground, the rhizomes are boiled, then dried and peeled, after which they are ground to a fine powder.

Right:
Turmeric being ground on the Plaine de Grêques on Réunion.

The turmeric plant has large, flat leaves that cluster round a central stem. This bears yellow flowers that are similar to those of lilies or of arum lilies. The plant thrives in hot climates, and favours deep, moist ground. It is propagated by dividing the rhizome.

FLAVOUR AND COLOUR

Like ginger and iris, turmeric develops an underground rhizome, a long, horizontal root-stem that puts out secondary roots under the ground and green shoots above. The rhizome is harvested, boiled, dried and peeled, then ground to a fine powder and is used to flavour all kinds of food, including preserves, vegetables, rice and a wide range of Eastern and African dishes.
This spice has a peppery, piquant and slightly bitter flavour. As with all other spices, it is best to buy whole turmeric rhizomes and to keep them in a cool, dark place. They should be peeled and ground to a powder just before use. Turmeric will also stain your hands, so it is advisable to wear gloves when you handle it. Both as a dye and as a flavouring, turmeric is a very acceptable substitute for saffron, and much less expensive.

Above:
Indian curry powder in an old-fashioned grocer's spice box.

Right:
A fresh sprig of the Indian curry plant *Murraya koenigii*, whose ground leaves are an ingredient of curry powder.

Curry

The word *curry* has three different meanings. It is the popular name for *Murraya koenigii*, a plant that grows in India and whose leaves are an ingredient of curry powder. The word also denotes the spicy powder that flavours curries, such as chicken, fish, prawn or vegetable curries. Although recipes for Indian curry powders vary according to region, the basic ingredients of all curry powders consist of turmeric, coriander, mustard, fenugreek, pepper, cumin, ginger and fresh curry leaves.

Ginger

The virtues of ginger have been known since ancient times. Writing in the first century AD the Greek physician and botanist Dioscorides described its medicinal virtues in De Materia Medica, *his treatise on medicine. Ginger and its uses as a spice were mentioned by Marco Polo, one of the first Europeans to set eyes on this plant, during his travels in China and Bengal during the 13th century.*

STRANGE SHAPES

Ginger, *Zingiber officinale*, is an attractive rhizomatous perennial. It has reed-like stems and leaves, and spiky yellow and purple flowers that are somewhat similar to gladioli.

The part of the plant that is used as a spice is the rhizome, a thick, fleshy underground stem that grows into strange shapes and has a hot, pungent taste.

Ginger is grown in tropical regions, most especially those of India, China and Japan, and also in Jamaica and in Queensland, northern Australia. It needs a hot, wet climate, and prefers a rich, humid and well-drained soil.

Propagation is by division of the rhizome. Newly divided rhizomes are planted in the spring and pulled up the following February, before new shoots start to grow. The harvested rhizomes are cleaned, peeled, washed and dried in the sun.

Above: Crystallized ginger packaged in China. In this form it can be used in confectionery or enjoyed as a sweet.

Left: The plump, knobbly ginger root grows vigorously, forming strange shapes. It has a pungent, fiery flavour.

IN ALL ITS FORMS

Ginger has a strong, fiery flavour and can be used in savoury as well as sweet dishes. While in Eastern cookery ginger is used to flavour sweet-and-sour dishes, in the West it is most often used in powdered form in cakes, and particularly to make gingerbread. It can also be used fresh and thinly sliced, as in Japanese cuisine, or dried, ground, preserved in syrup or crystallized. Ground ginger is also an ingredient of curry powder, and is particularly effective if it is freshly ground.

Gingembre Sauuage

Marco Polo

Marco Polo (1254–1324) was born into a wealthy family of Venetian spice merchants and spent most of his life travelling in India and the Far East. In 1271, at the age of 17, he set off on a journey to China and India with his father and his uncle. Leaving them to take care of trading activities, Marco Polo remained for 16 years in the service of Ghengis Khan in Beijing and carried out many missions. Taken prisoner during a naval battle in 1296, he was imprisoned in Genoa for four years. It was during this time that he dictated the enthralling account of his travels, known to us today as the *Travels of Marco Polo*.

Left:
Wild ginger depicted in an 18th-century engraving. Chinese ginger comes from the root of a related plant, *Lapinia officinalis*.

Above:
Marco Polo setting out from Venice with his father and uncle on a journey to Asia, the aim of which was to purchase spices. This illustration is from the *Travels of Marco Polo*, the detailed account of his journey to China and the 16-odd years that he spent there.

Nutmeg and mace

'Do you like nutmeg? It's been planted all over the place,' wrote the French writer Nicolas Boileau (1636–1711). This observation gives some idea of the popularity of this spice from as early as the Middle Ages. The tree that Boileau was writing about is Myristica fragrans, *which in fact produces two spices: nutmeg, the kernel of its seed, and mace, the seed's fibrous covering.*

NUTMEG IN THE SPICE WARS

The nutmeg tree is indigenous to the Moluccas, islands in eastern Indonesia. The Portuguese reached Indonesia in the 16th century, but control of the archipelago later passed to the Dutch, who held it for 200 years. For economic gain, the British seized control of Indonesia at the beginning of the 19th century. Like the Dutch before them, their aim was to gain exclusive control of Indonesia's plantations of clove and nutmeg trees, and thus to their yield of these highly prized spices. However, control of the Moluccas soon passed back to the Dutch, who held the islands until 1864, when the monopoly over the nutmeg trade was broken.

In the 18th century, the Frenchman Pierre Poivre (see page 29) established nutmeg plantations in Mauritius and Réunion. At a time when the Western world was gripped by spice fever, he braved considerable dangers to reach the Moluccas and steal a handful of nutmeg seedlings from the Dutch. With them he established new plantations, so that nutmeg became accessible to the whole world. Today, there are extensive nutmeg plantations in Sri Lanka, Malaysia and the West Indies.

Nutmeg kernels
are enclosed in an
oval shell, which
is in turn covered
by a fibrous
filigree coating,
known as mace.
Both the kernel
and the mace are
used as spices.

The nutmeg grater was once a very important piece of kitchen equipment. This is because, to bring out its full flavour, the kernel must be grated immediately before it is added to a dish. Today whole nutmeg is often sold with a miniature grater included in the packaging.

Below, left:
A nutmeg grater that slides into a drawer for storing whole nutmeg.

A TROPICAL TREE

The nutmeg is a fine evergreen tree that grows in a pyramidal shape up to a height of about 10 metres (33 feet). It has large, oval, elegantly tapering dark green leaves, which are also very aromatic. Like lemon trees, the nutmeg tree blooms all year round. It has white flowers, which produce orange-hued fruit similar to apricots. The tree thrives only in hot climates, and demands moist but well-drained soil that is rich in nutrients, light and sheltered from sun and wind. Ideal conditions for the nutmeg are similar to those that suit azaleas, camellias, hydrangeas and rhododendrons, though a tropical climate is essential.

Only the female plants produce fruit, which they start to bear after seven or eight years' growth. At maturity, which they reach after about 15 years, nutmeg trees may bear more than 2,000 fruit each year, and continue to be productive until they are over 80 years old. When the fruits are ripe they burst open, releasing the nut. The mace, which encases the shell, is removed and the shell is cracked to release the kernel. Both the kernel and the mace are then dried.

A WARM, RICH FLAVOUR

Nutmeg and mace are used to flavour both savoury and sweet dishes. They can either be ground or grated, but this should be done just before they are added to a dish as they quickly lose their flavour. This explains why nutmeg graters are so commonly found in collections of old kitchen

equipment and why whole
nutmeg is so often sold
with little graters
incorporated into the
packaging today. Added
just before serving, a little
nutmeg or mace will spice
up a béchamel sauce, a
quiche, a cheese soufflé,
creamed potatoes, pasta,
an omelette or soup.
Nutmeg or mace can also be
used to flavour gingerbread, apple pie or fruit salad.
Nutmeg and mace are also important in the perfume
industry. Both are used as ingredients of scent and
such products as toilet soaps and shampoos. In the past
nutmeg and mace were used in folk remedies, as they were
believed to cure rheumatism and respiratory
ailments. However, since strong doses of
nutmeg and mace can be harmful, they
should not be taken as medicines without
proper advice.

Above:
Cracking open the nutmeg's shell
reveals the kernel. Mace, the
fibrous network covering the
shell, is also used as a spice.

Pierre Poivre

The doyen of the spice trade in the 18th century was the Frenchman Pierre Poivre (1719–86). By strange coincidence, his name translates as Peter Pepper, although there is no connection between him and the origin of the word pepper.
Pierre Poivre led a remarkably eventful life. He was born in Lyon and had early ambitions to join the priesthood, but instead embarked on several long and perilous sea voyages. He then turned to natural history, to which he devoted the rest of his life. He joined the French East India Company in 1749.
Pierre Poivre travelled all over the world in search of spices and pioneered the cultivation of cloves, nutmeg and other spices. He established plantations on the Île de France and Île de Bourbon, now known as Mauritius and Réunion respectively.
In Mauritius Pierre Poivre created the Jardin des Pamplemousses (Grapefuit Garden), containing not only many varieties of plants but also several species of animals.

Pepper

Pepper is harvested at various stages of ripeness, just as olives are. Green pepper is picked before the berries have completely ripened and red pepper when the berries are fully ripe. This illustration, which shows pepper being harvested in southern India in the 13th century, is from the *Travels of Marco Polo*, an account of Polo's experiences in the Far East.

Of all spices, pepper is the most widely cultivated and the most commonly used in the world. Once highly prized, it was treated as a rare and precious commodity. Pepper has been the cause of wars and the purpose of distant journeys; it can even be said to have altered the course of history.

A SPICE USED AS CURRENCY

Pepper was once so expensive that dishonest merchants would pass off juniper berries as genuine peppercorns. In ancient Rome, especially deserving soldiers were paid in peppercorns and in the Middle Ages a man's wealth was measured in terms of his reserves of this precious spice. Pepper could also make up a dowry and could be used to pay taxes or rent. At this time pepper was used to flavour food but it was used most especially as a preservative. Later, as other spices arrived in Europe, pepper was less highly prized and, as it was more widely available, it even became commonplace. By the 19th century both salt and pepper were customary condiments on the dining table of every Western household.

Pepper was introduced into Europe by the Portuguese in the 16th century and they retained a monopoly of the pepper trade until the 18th century. It was thanks to Pierre Poivre, whose name uncannily translates as Peter Pepper (see page 29), that pepper reached the French colonies, as this great navigator established plantations on the islands of Mauritius and Réunion. Although pepper is indigenous to India, most especially to the Malabar Coast, today it is also grown in Indonesia, Sri Lanka, Brazil and Madagascar.

THE PEPPER VINE

Black pepper, or *Piper nigrum*, belongs to the Piperaceae family. It is a vine-like creeper that grows wild in the moist, equatorial regions of India.

It puts out supple stems similar to those of the vanilla plant and reaches a height of 6 metres (20 feet).

Its leaves are oval, tapering, veined and shiny. It has white flowers, which grow in grape-like clusters and which produce berries that turn from green to red as they ripen. Harvested and laid out on sheets to dry in the sun, the berries turn black.

The pepper plant and the various ways in which it is grown, is shown in an 18th-century engraving. It is propagated by taking cuttings, which are planted in a nursery. The young plants are then transferred to the plantation, where they are trained up a stake or a shrub, which also protects the vine from the searing heat of the sun. Although the vine can grow to a height of 6 metres (20 feet), it is trimmed to half its size to make it easier to harvest the berries. Each plant is productive for about ten years.

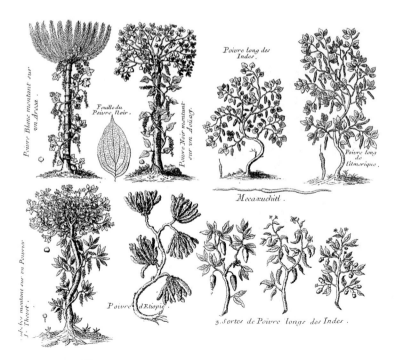

CULTIVATING THE PEPPER VINE

Because the pepper plant is a creeper with floppy branches it has to be grown with a stake. Hardwood stakes, or simply the trunk of a shrub planted at the same time, are used. The shrub must not take too much out of the soil and it must be suited to the same conditions, namely a rich, light soil, well watered and well drained. This method also gives the pepper plant shade, as *Piper nigrum* needs filtered light to develop its aroma. Moreover, the pepper plant is highly sensitive to wind, heavy rain and long periods of drought.

The pepper vine is propagated by taking cuttings. Runners about 50 cm long are cut and planted in a nursery, in the shade, where they quickly take root. The young plants are then transferred to the plantation, where they are planted next to stakes. When the stem has grown to 2–3 metres (6–10 feet), it is cut back to make it easier to harvest. The pepper is harvested three years later, and continues to be productive for about 12 years.

Sachets of peppercorns for sale in Izräel, the Parisian spice shop. Many different kinds of pepper are available here, including colourful pre-packaged mixtures of black, white, red and green peppercorns.

GREEN, BLACK AND WHITE PEPPERCORNS

Pepper is available as green, black or white corns. Green pepper is picked when the berries are still unripe and is used fresh rather than dried, either as individual grains or on the vine. It is slightly less fiery than other types of pepper, with a hint of sweetness. Black pepper is obtained by picking the grains when they are red and fully ripe, and by drying them in the sun for about a week. White pepper is obtained by soaking red grains in brine to remove their outer skin and drying them in the sun. White pepper has a sharper flavour than black but a slightly duller aroma.

Centre: Black, green and mixed peppercorns. Freshly ground pepper gives the fullest flavour.

Below: An old-fashioned pepper mill in the shape of a miniature coffee grinder.

Right: Freshly harvested green pepper on the vine is available from certain specialist outlets.

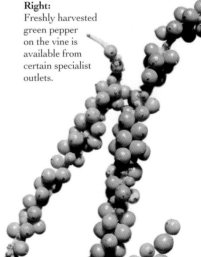

Above: Drying peppercorns at a plantation in the Amazon, Brazil. Picked when they are red, they are exposed to the sun and turn dark brown as they dry.

Right: Herbs and spices were once valued as much for their medicinal properties as for their culinary uses. Thus there was little distinction between herbalists, apothecaries and spice sellers.

ANISE PEPPER AND LONG PEPPER

There are other kinds of pepper, but these do not come from the pepper vine *Piper nigrum*.

Anise pepper, also known as Szechuan pepper, is the berry of a spiny type of ash tree, *Zanthoxylum piperitum*. It is stronger than green, black or white pepper, with a hint of lemon and aniseed. Long pepper comes from *Piper longum*, a creeper with large oval fruit. This type of pepper was widely used in ancient Greek and

Roman times but was gradually forgotten as the berries of *Piper nigrum*, familiar to us today, became more popular. Long pepper is almost impossible to buy, except in some highly specialized outlets. It has a slightly sweet aroma, and is less pungent than *Piper nigrum*.

Pepper is the most popular spice in the world, and it is used to season all kinds of sweet and savoury dishes. Like most other spices, it should be ground just before use so that it imparts its full flavour. This is why pepper mills not only have a grinding device but also a compartment to hold a small number of whole peppercorns. The best pepper mills are made of wood as, like most other spices, peppercorns keep best in containers made of natural materials.

Spices for health

Although pepper is used primarily as a spice, it also has curative properties. It aids digestion, stimulates the appetite and calms nausea. Many other spices also have therapeutic qualities. In ancient Greece and Rome, and in medieval Italy, for example, spices were customarily used to cure a wide range of ailments. Although their health-restoring virtues have now largely been forgotten, spices are used in the manufacture of certain modern medicines.

Fragrant essential oils extracted from spices are, however, used in aromatherapy. Dill is a mild sedative and is also an effective cure for digestive troubles. Cinnamon is a remedy for colds and chills and a tonic for those involved in strenuous sports. Cloves revitalize the nervous system. Juniper berries have disinfectant properties and can also be taken as a diuretic and purgative. Spices have many other medicinal uses.

Mediterranean spices

*S*pices such as anise, mustard and fenugreek, have been part of Western cuisine for thousands of years. The ancient Greeks and Romans valued them for their aroma. Later, these herbs were cultivated by monks, who tended them in their gardens. Like Eastern spices, Mediterranean spices have a huge range of flavours, and can be used in both sweet and savoury dishes.

Anise

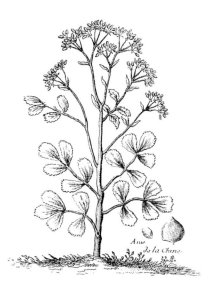

This elegant annual came originally from Greece and Egypt. It belongs to the Umbelliferae, *a family of plants with umbrella-shaped flowerheads. This family includes many other aromatic plants, among them parsley, fennel, dill, coriander, cumin, curry and chervil.*

DELICATE FLOWERHEADS

Anise, *Pimpinella anisum*, is an umbellifer, or a member of the parsley family. It is an annual with bright green serrated leaves and long, slender stems and white umbels, or flowerheads with radiating stalks. When it is in flower the plant can stand 60–70 cm (24–27 inches) high. It is self-seeding in its indigenous habitat but it is easy to grow in any well-drained soil in a sunny situation, although the seeds will only ripen in a warm climate. Other plants of the parsley family can, however, be grown very easily in northern Europe.

MEDICINAL USES

Since ancient times, the seeds of the anise plant, or aniseed, have been used for their medicinal properties. Writing in the first century AD, the Greek physician Dioscorides described the healing virtues of anise. Aniseed essence relieves digestive problems and aids digestion, and chewing the seeds sweetens the breath.

Above:
An 18th-century engraving of an anise plant, showing its large, elegant flowerheads.

Right:
The aniseed sweets made at the Abbaye de Flavigny, in France, consist of anise seeds coated in thin layers of sugar. They have been made at the abbey for hundreds of years.

A HEADY AROMA

It is best to buy anise in the form of whole seeds and to crush them just before use in order to bring out their full flavour. In Indian cuisine and in Mediterranean countries, anise is added to savoury dishes, such as fish soup. Anise seeds can also be added to herbal teas, and can be sprinkled over a green salad or a fruit salad. They can be incorporated into cake mixtures and ice-cream mixtures.

A few grains of aniseed also add extra flavour to such quintessential Mediterranean drinks as anisette, ouzo and pastis. Aniseed is a delicious spice with a sweet, heady aroma, but the leaves of the anise plant can also be used as a herb. Both aniseed and fresh anise leaves can be found in specialist shops. However, the leaves do not keep well, so it is best to buy small quantities at a time and use them within a few days.

Anise seeds, freshly harvested from the plant. They keep well if stored in a cool, dark place but should be crushed just before use to release their full flavour.

Pastis

The aniseed-flavoured alcoholic drink, pastis, has a distinctive aroma redolent of the warmth and voluptuousness of southern France. The word *pastis* probably comes from a local slang word meaning mess, chaos or general disorder. It was probably adopted because pastis turns cloudy when water is added to it. Ricard, famously marketed as '*le vrais pastis de Marseille*', or the only genuine Marseille pastis, was invented in the early 1930s by Paul Ricard. Until then, pastis had been a bland drink, with a low alcohol content. Paul Ricard's new recipe consisted of a mixture of anise, star anise and liquorice macerated in alcohol. In 1938 the legally permitted alcohol content of pastis was increased, as was the proportion of anise. Pastis with its familiar aroma and fully rounded flavour was born and became an internationally popular drink.

Coriander (Cilantro)

Like anise, coriander belongs to the parsley family, the Umbelliferae. *Although fresh coriander leaves have a rather harsh flavour, coriander seeds are one of the most subtly flavoured of all spices.*

A HERB AND A SPICE

Coriander, or cilantro, has been used as a herb and a spice since ancient times. In his *Natural History*, the Roman writer Pliny the Elder (AD 23–79) extolled the virtues of a variety of coriander grown in Egypt. Coriander, or *Coriandrum sativum*, grows in slightly different ways and develops slightly different flavours depending on the soil and climate. It thrives in any well-drained soil but needs warmth and sunlight. It has pink and white flowers, which grow on stems up to 50 cm (20 inches) tall. Coriander blooms in summer and its seeds are harvested before they are completely ripe. As coriander is self-seeding, it can be left to go to seed. Alternatively, the seeds can be sown in the autumn.

Coriander, also known as dizzycorn, is a delicate, fine-stemmed plant with pink and white flat-topped flowerheads. Although the leaves have a powerful aroma similar to the odour given off by stink bugs, their flavour is surprisingly subtle. Finely chopped, they can be used as aromatic herbs.

A SUBTLE FLAVOUR

The coriander plant has a strong smell similar to that given off by stink bugs. In fact the word coriander comes from *koros*, the ancient Greek word for stink bug. Ripe coriander seeds, by contrast, have a delicate, lightly pungent flavour reminiscent of orange zest, which grows more rounded with time. Freshly ground or freshly crushed, so that they lose none of their flavour, coriander seeds are used in savoury dishes, such as meat balls and salads, and also in sweet dishes like cakes, creams and ice-cream mixtures. Powdered coriander seeds, which are classed as a spice, or finely chopped fresh coriander leaves, which are aromatic herbs, can be added to soups or vegetables *au gratin*. The leaves can also be sprinkled on a bowl of pumpkin soup or chopped into steamed and sautéd carrots.

Coriander seeds are the shape and size of peppercorns. Dry-roasting them in a pan before they are ground or crushed and added to food brings out their flavour, which has a strong hint of orange zest.

Harissa

Made with red chilli peppers, harissa is hot, spicy condiment that is particularly popular in Moroccan, Algerian and Tunisian cuisine. In this recipe proportions can be varied according to taste.

10–30 small red chilli peppers
2 tablespoons of coriander seeds
2 tablespoons of cumin seeds
2 cloves of garlic
olive oil
salt

Cut the chilli peppers in half lengthwise and remove the seeds. Chop them and boil in water for 20 minutes. Grind the coriander and cumin seeds and toast them in a frying pan. Crush the garlic. Then mix the chilli peppers, garlic and spices together, season with salt and add enough olive oil to produce the desired consistency.

Cumin

While many spices were introduced to Europe from the East, cumin, which is indigenous to Mediterranean countries, has been avidly adopted by Chinese, Indonesian and Indian cuisine.

Cumin is a very popular spice in northern Europe. Gouda with cumin seeds is a traditional Dutch speciality.

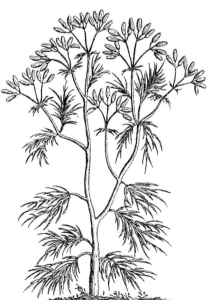

MINUTE SEEDS

Cumin, or *Cuminum cyminum*, is an ancient culinary spice and is mentioned in St Mark's Gospel. The plant, a member of the parsley family, is a small annual with serrated leaves and white umbrella-shaped flowerheads that produce very small, slender seeds. In flower, the plant grows no more than about 30 cm (12 inches) tall. It needs a mild climate, well-drained soil and a sunny position. The seeds are harvested before they are fully ripe. The seedheads are cut and winnowed to extract the seeds, which are spread out to dry in the sun.

A BITTERSWEET FLAVOUR

Cumin seeds are used either whole or ground. They have a bitter although warm and somewhat sweet flavour. There are two varieties, white cumin and black cumin. The latter has an even subtler, sweeter flavour, and the seeds are smaller. As with all spices, cumin seeds should be kept in an airtight container, in a dark place. They should be ground or dry-roasted in a frying plan immediately before they are used. Cumin seeds have a very pervasive flavour, which is still recognizable when they are mixed with other spices or flavours. Because of this, cumin should only be used in small quantities.

Cumin is closely associated with Indian cookery; it is an ingredient of garam masala, for example. It is also used in Arabic and Turkish cuisine. In Germany cumin seeds are mixed into bread dough.

Cumin lassi

Lassi is a traditional Indian drink. It comes from the Punjab, in northern India.

It is easy to make at home. Salt lassi can be served with a main course or a salad, and sweet lassi goes well with desserts.

Serves 4
4 natural yogurts
half a cup of ice-cold water
salt and/or sugar
4 tablespoons of cumin seeds
(or other suitable ground spices)

Pour all the ingredients into a large bowl and beat the mixture with a whisk. Serve the lassi ice-cold or add a few ice cubes.

Spice shops

*O*ld-fashioned grocers' shops, with their aroma of roasted coffee, tea and *fresh fruit, and stacked with jute sacks of nuts and pulses and tins of aromatic spices, are almost unknown today. Their nearest approximation are health-food shops, certain specialist stores and the family-run Indian and Chinese shops that are to be found in large towns and cities.*

Wealthy merchants

In the Middle Ages there was very little distinction between spice sellers and apothecaries. Both sold all manner of spices and aromatic herbs, which were regarded both as culinary delicacies and as medicinal remedies. Later the two trades diverged. Selling spices, as opposed to providing medical preparations, became a separate trade, and one that brought certain merchants great wealth.

At the end of the 19th century shops specializing exclusively in spices were rare. Today they have been largely replaced by health-food shops and by small family-run establishments selling Chinese and Indian spices. Here, something of the colour, aroma and flavour of old-fashioned spice shops has been preserved.

The role of spices

At that time, spices were used as much to flavour dishes as to mask the taste of food that had become rank because there was no satisfactory way of preserving it.

In the past, the term 'spice' was also used for all kinds of sweet things simply because confectionery, jam and crystallized fruit were prepared with spices as a matter of course. In France up until the Revolution, the word 'spice' also designated lawyers' payment because of the ancient custom of paying them in spices, that is, in cakes and sweet foods.

Above: Izraël, in the Marais district of Paris, is one of the last surviving shops in Europe that is devoted exclusively to spices.
Below: an Indian spice shop.

Buying spices

Today it is increasingly difficult to buy unpackaged spices, especially raw spices that one can process at home. Most health-food shops offer a relatively wide range of spices, which are either sold loose or packaged. Some larger supermarkets also carry a good range of spices, although these are more likely to be packaged. Izraël, in the Marais district of Paris, is one of the few remaining high-class spice shops with a very wide choice of goods. It stocks virtually every type of spice from every corner of the world, with a panoply of colours and aromas. Here spices are sold either loose, in tall glass jars, or packed and in sachets. Mixtures of spices are also available here, either ready-packaged or prepared to individual requirements. Shops selling Moroccan, West Indian, Chinese and Indian foods are also good sources, as spices are an integral part of the cuisine of those regions. Ideally it is best to buy spices in their unprocessed form – that is, as whole grains and berries, roots or bark – and to grind or chop them just before you use them so that they release all of their wonderful flavours.

Spice mixtures

Certain inspired combinations of spices can transform a dish. While certain spice mixtures are an integral part of a country's cuisine, you can also create your own mixtures, according to personal taste or to a favourite dish.

Preceding pages:
A spice souk in Taroudant, Morocco.
Below:
A selection of different spices and Guyanese peppers.
Right:
Garam masala is an Indian spice mixture. It consists of bay leaves, cloves, cinnamon, coriander, pepper, cumin, cardamom and star anise.

INDIA

Indian cooks use a particularly large repertoire of spice mixtures, the best-known of which are curry powder and garam masala. However, the precise ingredients of these mixtures vary considerably depending on the region and the cook's own personal taste. There is a great variety of Indian spice mixtures. Most are easy to prepare and can be used in Western dishes. One such spice mixtures is *panch phoran*, the main ingredients of which are whole cumin, fennel, mustard, fenugreek and nigella seeds. This mixture imparts a delicious flavour to vegetable dishes.

INDONESIA

Various spice mixtures are also used in Indonesian cuisine. The most popular is sambal, which is made from peppers (500 grams of sweet red peppers, 2 teaspoons of salt and 2 teaspoons of sugar). It is easy to prepare: simply boil the peppers in water, drain and purée them. Then add the salt and sugar. Sambal is a condiment that is used in the same way as mustard. It is used as an accompaniment to a main dish, such as fish served with vegetables.

AFRICA

In African cuisine, Harissa is a Tunisian spice mixture that is most often eaten with couscous. *Ras el-hanout* is its Moroccan equivalent. The main ingredients of these mixtures are cardamom, mace, pepper, nutmeg, cinnamon, cloves and love-in-a-mist seeds, together with flowers such as rose buds and lavender pods.

CHINA

The best-known Chinese spice mixture is five-spice powder, which is used as an accompaniment to duck and pork. It consists of star anise, pepper, cinnamon, fennel seed and cloves and is prepared simply by grinding these ingredients and mixing them all together.

EUROPE

European cuisine has appropriated and adapted an international range of spice mixtures. Although spice mixtures can easily be prepared at home, many delicious mixtures are available from specialist spice shops. Some will even prepare mixtures to meet customers' individual requirements. Aromatic herbs can also be incorporated into spice mixtures.

Panch phoran is an Indian spice mixture that is used to flavour vegetable dishes. It consists of cumin, fennel, mustard, fenugreek and love-in-a-mist seeds.

Three spice mixtures

• The following spice mixture can be used to flavour casseroles and rice dishes. It can also be sprinkled over meat and fish: garlic, semolina, paprika, ground black pepper, ground Cayenne pepper, thyme, oregano and salt.

• For grilled meat: ground black pepper, ground celery seeds, Cayenne pepper, thyme, marjoram, paprika, ground mustard and salt.

• The following traditional British mixture is used to flavour desserts, cakes and biscuits, as well as in recipes or to decorate cakes and desserts: whole coriander seeds, pieces of cinnamon, whole peppers, cloves, and ground nutmeg and ginger.

Fenugreek

Fenugreek, whose scientific name means 'Greek hay', is a delicate spice with an aroma similar to that of celery. The plant itself has the smell of freshly mown hay. Rich in minerals, vitamins and proteins, fenugreek is also used as a tonic.

A VERSATILE PLANT

Fenugreek, or *Trigonella foenum-graecum*, is a small leguminous plant that thrives in warm, dry climates, It grows in the wild in Mediterranean regions. It has vertical stems that grow no higher than 10–20 cm (4–8 inches) high, depending on the soil in which the plant takes root. It has green, lobe-like leaves with a slightly toothed margin, and its flowers are yellowish-white. The flowers produce pointed pods that contain small square seeds; these are used as a spice. The scientific name for fenugreek means 'Greek hay'. One explanation for this is that the plant smells of freshly cut hay but this name may also be connected to the fact that in the Mediterranean basin fenugreek is grown as a high-energy feed for horses. For humans, fenugreek is effective in boosting metabolism and for curing anaemia. The plant also produces a yellow dye for textiles.

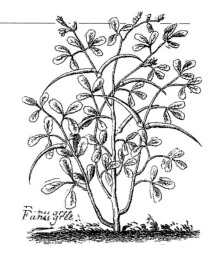

Right:
Fenugreek seeds have a celery-like aroma. They are brown and square and are contained within slender, curved pods.

Top right:
The fenugreek plant, illustrated in this 17th-century engraving, is a small annual that grows no higher than 15 cm (6 inches) tall. The seeds are used as a spice and the leaves as aromatic herbs. The young shoots can be eaten in salads.

HERB AND SPICE

Fresh fenugreek leaves, which have a bitter taste, can be used as a herb. The seeds, which should be ground just before use, are similarly bitter-tasting but also have an exquisite celery-like aroma.

Although fenugreek is not widely used in Western cuisine, it is an important spice in African and Indian dishes.

It is an ingredient of certain spice mixtures, most especially curry mixtures.

Fenugreek is also an aromatic herb. Finely chopped, fresh fenugreek leaves will impart their distinctive slightly bitter, celery-like flavour to salads as well as to carrots, cauliflower or potatoes cooked *au gratin*.

Fenugreek is an ingredient of many Indian spice mixtures, including *pan massala* (**right**) which is served as an appetizer. Although fenugreek seeds are hard and therefore difficult to grind, they are an ingredient of most of the Indian spice mixtures used to prepare curry.

Spices in Indian cuisine

Spices are an integral part of Indian food, and delicious Indian spice mixtures, such as curry powder, or massala, exist in almost endless variations. In a traditional Indian curry a spice mixture should penetrate the dish in such a way that the individual flavours of the spices cannot be distinguished. Indian spice mixtures can be sweet and mild, sharp, warm and pungent, or hot and searing. Curry is predominantly a southern Indian dish, and garam massala more typical of northern India. This spice mixture consists of cinnamon, cumin, coriander, cardamom, pepper, cloves and mace. Meat dishes are also more characteristic of northern India, while dishes of rice and vegetables flavoured with spices are more typical of southern India.

Mustard

Used since time immemorial, today this spice is a ubiquitous condiment. Besides mustard in its classic guises, there are also more elaborate varieties, ready-mixed or to be prepared at home.

Common mustard is a plant often found in the countryside today, and its white form, *Sinapsis alba*, is used as an aromatic herb. It can also be grown easily in a pot.

Opposite:
A field of mustard beginning to go to seed.

TYPES OF MUSTARD

Mustard belongs to the *Cruciferae*, a family of annuals that also includes cabbage, cauliflower and turnip. Three varieties of mustard plant are used to produce the condiment.

Brown mustard, or *Brassica juncea*, has yellow flowers and small brown seeds. It grows to a height of 1.2–1.5 metres (4–5 feet). The seeds, which have a fiery flavour, are easy to harvest. Today this variety is extensively grown to make mustard.

Black mustard, or *Brassica nigra*, is the most common variety. It rarely grows more than 1 metre (3 feet) high and flourishes on country roadsides. Although it originated in the

Several different types of mustard can be made by mixing ground mustard seeds with white or red wine and spices. Any type of mustard can also be flavoured in different ways by the addition of other spices.

Left, clockwise from bottom: mustard with whole spice seeds; with red mustard seeds and with green mustard seeds.

Flavoured mustard

Prepared mustard is sold in many different flavours. The French brand Maille, for example, produces mustards with a range of flavours, including raspberry, cognac, champagne, walnut, rosehip, herb, green pepper and tarragon. Flavoured mustards are very easy to make at home. Spices such as ginger, peppers, anise or horseradish, either used singly or in combinations, can be stirred in to mustard. Mustard mixed with crème fraîche produces a delicious mustard sauce that makes an ideal accompaniment to fish, seafood or mixed vegetables.

Mediterranean basin, it spread throughout all but the northernmost regions of Europe. As a result of human migration it now also grows in America and Asia. Black mustard, which is referred to as wild mustard in the Gospels, was originally a medicinal plant, used as an emetic and to relieve inflammation. From the 13th century it was used as a condiment. As it is very strong, black mustard is less popular than other varieties. It has, however, become a common ingredient of Indian cuisine and is used in many Indian dishes.

White mustard, or *Sinapis alba* (also known as *Brassica birta*), grows no taller than 30–40 cm (12–16 inches) high. While its seeds are used to make the condiment, it is also a medicinal plant as it is used to make mustard poultices.

Left:
Black mustard seeds produce the strongest mustard.

Above:
A tin of Colman's mustard. English mustard consists of white mustard powder mixed with flour.

CLASSIC VARIETIES OF MUSTARD

English mustard, which is bright yellow, is the most finely ground of all mustards and the one with the strongest taste. The finely ground powder is mixed with water, milk or beer to form a smooth paste. It is also available ready-mixed.

French Dijon mustard, which is a deep golden yellow, is a fine smooth paste that consists of ground mustard seeds mixed with white wine and spices. It has a mellow taste.

Beaujolais mustard, which contains red wine, has a less refined texture than Dijon mustard. The wine gives it a reddish hue.

Meaux mustard, which contains less finely ground seeds, is even coarser. It is less hot than the Dijon and Beaujolais varieties and is less spicy, although it has a more rounded flavour.

Mustard was traditionally sold and kept in small stoneware pots made in a variety of different shapes.

18th-century mustard pots from the collection of the French makers Maille, one of the oldest makers of Dijon mustard.

The modern method of making Dijon mustard was invented by a Mrs Clements, from Durham, in the north of England, in the late 18th century.

Spices from the New World

*C*hristopher Columbus set out aboard the Santa Maria *to find a more direct route to the East, and thus to a wealth of Eastern spices. Instead, having crossed the Atlantic, he reached Cuba and Haiti, then sailed further eastwards to the coast of Central America and the islands which he named the West Indies. Thanks to him, Europeans were introduced to chilli peppers, allspice and vanilla, as well as other foodstuffs.*

Peppers

Christopher Columbus returned from the New World with a cargo of exotic plants. Among them were peppers, which were a revelation to European palates. The inhabitants of the New World, however, had been using them for thousands of years, both as a spice and as a medicine.

There are many different types of pepper, each with a different shape and flavour.
Right: Dried African chilli peppers, a long, thin variety.
Above and opposite page: Fresh green and red sweet peppers.

FROM THE NEW WORLD

Scholarly research on the history of plants in human civilization has established that peppers were unknown to the ancient Greeks, Romans, Hebrews or Chinese, none of whom ever mentioned them in their writings. Peppers, which are indigenous exclusively to Central and South America, probably originated in Brazil. In the 15th century, after the Europeans had discovered the New World, peppers were brought back to Europe and began to be grown in Europe and Asia. Today, peppers are commercially grown not only in the United States and in Mexico but also in Hungary, Spain, Italy and France. The small town of Espelette, in the Basque region of France, has become famous for its red peppers.

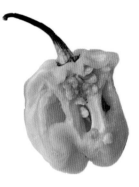

GROWING, HARVESTING AND DRYING

Like tomatoes and potatoes, peppers belong to the *Solanacea* family. There are over 200 varieties, but only two are extensively cultivated: these are the sweet pepper, *Capsicum annuum*, and the chilli pepper, *Capsicum frutescens*. Chilli peppers, also known as Cayenne chillies, are very hot.

Peppers are extensively cultivated in tropical regions of the world where the soil is rich and fertile and where there is plenty of rainfall. Peppers can also be grown in Europe, but they are treated as an annual rather than as a perennial, and are often cultivated under cover. Seeds are sown in a nursery in the spring, when temperatures begin to rise, thus encouraging germination. The seedlings are then planted out in rows, 60 cm (2 feet) apart. About three months after sowing, the plants have produced fruits, which start to turn red. These are picked by hand, so that the stalk remains on each pepper. The peppers are sorted, and any damaged or rotten fruit is discarded. They are then sun-dried in the open air, the traditional method being to thread them on to strings that are hung on a line suspended between two posts. As they lose their moisture, the peppers shrink and wrinkle but continue to ripen. They are then heated in an oven, after which some are sold whole and others are ground to powder.

FRESH PEPPERS

Peppers can also be used when they are fresh. Several varieties of freshly picked peppers, each of which vary in strength, are available in supermarkets and greengrocers.

Espelette peppers

Espelette, a small town in the Basque region of France, is famous for its sweet red peppers, or 'piments basquais'. The façades of houses there are covered with strings of peppers, slowly drying in the sun.

Red peppers, or *Capsicum annuum*, reached this part of southwestern France in the 16th century, having been brought back to Spain from the New World. Espelette peppers, which thrive in this hot, humid region of France, are a local speciality. These dried peppers can be ground, made into a sauce or a purée or mixed with vinegar.

Right: Tinned sweet red peppers of the kind used to make paprika, an important ingredient in Hungarian cuisine. The particular variety used is *Capsicum tetragonum*, which is ground to a powder. One of its principal uses is in goulash.

Far right: A garland of dried red peppers.

Below: Espelette peppers are hung out to dry on lengths of string suspended from the façades of houses, and are then stored in large wicker baskets.

Opposite page: Peppers can also be eaten fresh. Because much of the heat of chilli peppers is contained in their seeds, it is often best to remove these. Large sweet peppers can be stuffed.

Serrano chillies may be green or red. While the green ones are hot, the red ones are sweet. Chillies, from California, can be green or dark red and are quite sweet. The best-known are Cayenne chillies, which are small, long and thin. These have a fiery heat. When handling hot chillies, wear rubber gloves and take care not to touch your eyes or mouth. Removing the seeds will make then less searing. Chillies can be added to a ratatouille, puréed and added to rice or savoury semolina dishes.

DRIED PEPPERS
Because they keep well, dried peppers are easy to use. Several different varieties of dried chillies are also available, with a range of different strengths and flavours, from very mild to extremely hot. Ancho chillies are short and plump, with a gentle, fruity flavour. Tepin chillies are very small, with a mild walnut flavour. Cayenne chillies, which are usually sold in powdered form as Cayenne pepper, have a very strong, fiery flavour and should be used in small quantities and with care. All types of peppers and chillies can be toasted under the grill then ground. In powdered form they can be added to fresh or dried vegetables, and can also be mixed with other spices such as cumin, pepper or coriander.

Allspice

Allspice, also known as pimento or Jamaican pepper, has the appearance of large peppercorns. As its name implies, it has the flavour of several different spices, namely pepper, cloves, nutmeg and cinnamon.

Scallops with allspice

8 scallops
25 grams of butter
2 shallots
half a glass of white wine
the juice of 1 lemon
2 spoonfuls of crème fraîche
allspice

Cook the scallops in stock. To make the sauce, finely chop the shallots and mix them with the melted butter, the wine, the lemon juice and the crème fraîche. Add the allspice to taste. Arrange the scallops on plates and pour the sauce over them.

FRUIT OF AN ELEGANT TREE

The elegant allspice tree, *Pimenta officinalis*, belongs to the myrtle family. Indigenous to Central America, it is an evergreen tree that grows to a height of 10 metres (33 feet). It has thick, oily leaves and its grey bark has a strong aroma. The flowers, which develop at the end of the branches, are greenish-white and have a sweet and intense scent. The flowers produce succulent dark purple berries, which can be used fresh but which are more usually dried. Many of the world's largest allspice plantations are in Jamaica, where the tree thrives in ordinary, or even poor, soil, so long as it is well drained.

ALLSPICE IN SWEET AND SAVOURY DISHES

Allspice has an exquisite flavour, which can best be described as a blend of cinnamon, cloves and nutmeg, hence its name. Allspice goes very well with fish, shellfish and vegetables, and can also be added to cake mixtures, creams and pancake mixture. It can also be stirred into drinks, including orange squash and mulled wine, and blended into mayonnaise or vinaigrette dressings.

Dried allspice, like the dried berries of other spice plants, keeps very well in an airtight container stored in a cool, dark place. It will release maximum flavour if crushed or ground just before use.

Left:
An 18th-century engraving depicting an envoy of the Spanish crown arresting Christopher Columbus at the time of his third voyage to the New World. Columbus was ordered to return to Spain, and the importance of his great discoveries was not recognized.

Opposite page:
Harvested while still green and turning a deep purple as they dry in the sun, allspice berries look like large peppercorns. They can be used in both sweet and savoury dishes, and impart the strongest flavour if they are crushed or ground just before use.

Above:
Christopher Columbus in an anonymous 16th-century portrait. Columbus sailed from Cadiz on 3rd August 1492 and, although he failed to find a sea route to India, he returned from his voyages to the West Indies and Central America with several newly discovered spices, including allspice.

One of the best and easiest ways of storing whole spices is in airtight containers like those in this set of stacking boxes. Spices should also be kept in a cool, dark place.

Preparing and storing spices

There are several ways of preparing spices to bring out their wonderful flavours. Many spices have already travelled halfway round the world before they are offered for sale in greengrocers and supermarkets but most keep well if they are properly stored.

• Grating

Many spices, such as nutmeg and ginger, do not release their flavour unless they are grated. Although a wide range of graters is specially designed for spices, you can use an ordinary cheese grater with different grades of perforations.

• Crushing

Juniper berries, ginger and cardamom seeds give much more flavour if they are ground or crushed in a mortar. Stone pestles and mortars suitable for preparing spices in this way are widely available. Many of them are made in India.

• Grinding

Ginger, mace, cinnamon and aromatic seeds can be used in powdered form. Ground spices can more easily be added to recipes and can also be sprinkled over dishes just before serving. The easiest way of grinding spices is in a small wooden spice mill, which is just like a miniature coffee grinder, or in an ordinary pepper mill or coffee grinder.

• Toasting

Certain aromatic seeds, such as coriander, release more of their subtle flavour if they are gently toasted in a frying pan. Do not add any oil but shake

Preparing spices

A few simple pieces of kitchen equipment will allow you to obtain the maximum flavour from your spices. With a grater, a pestle and mortar, a spice or pepper mill, a blender, a frying pan and some muslin, you can prepare different types of spices in many different ways, according to the dish or recipe.

the pan constantly to prevent the seeds from burning. They will fill the air with a delicious aroma. Crushed in a mortar, toasted spices can be incorporated into recipes or added to spice mixtures.

• Infusions

Certain spices make delicious and refreshing infusions. Anise, for example, steeped in boiling water makes a delicious hot drink and can also be added to a pot of tea, a hot toddy or mulled wine.

Remove the spice after a few minutes, or when it has imparted the desired amount of flavour.

Storing spices

Spices for every day use were traditionally kept in spice boxes with several compartments. Some antique spice boxes, particularly those made of silver or brass, are true works of art. A range of containers suitable for keeping spices is available today, including wooden boxes made in China or India. Less frequently used spices should be kept in a cool, dark place, in small jars or in china pots with airtight lids. Stored in an airtight container placed in the refrigerator, fresh spices, such as peppers, curry leaves or root ginger, will keep in a good condition for a week.

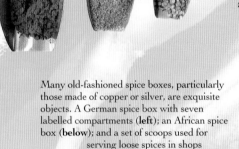

Many old-fashioned spice boxes, particularly those made of copper or silver, are exquisite objects. A German spice box with seven labelled compartments (**left**); an African spice box (**below**); and a set of scoops used for serving loose spices in shops (**above**).

Vanilla

Although it has a very pervasive flavour, vanilla is the sweetest and most delicate of all the spices. It goes very well with sweet dishes, and leading chefs now also use it in savoury dishes.

A TYPE OF ORCHID

Vanilla planifolia, the variety of vanilla used as a spice, is one of 64 different species of vanilla. A member of the orchid family, it is a climbing plant that is indigenous to the tropical regions of Mexico. The main stem puts out aerial roots, with which the plant attaches itself to a tree or other support. It grows near coasts, in equatorial forests or in any situation where it can climb up other plants, generally reaching great heights. It is an evergreen with greenish-white, orchid-like flowers that form long fleshy pods up to 10–15 cm (4–6 inches) long.

Neither the flower nor the fruit is scented. As the pods dry they wrinkle and crack, releasing the distinctive aroma of vanilla.

GROWING VANILLA

Vanilla is cultivated in hot, humid regions

Wild vanilla climbs up the branches of trees. Attaching itself with aerial roots, it reaches the very top of the forest canopy. Cultivated vanilla is trained up posts and is regularly trimmed.

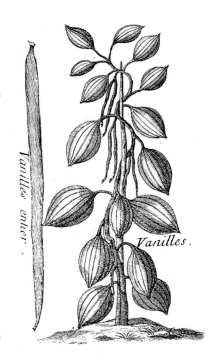

Vanilles entier.

Vanilles.

of the world, particularly in Madagascar, Tahiti and Réunion. It thrives in low-lying areas with rich soil but in plantations it needs a regular provision of fertilizer. The plant produces fruit from its fourth year and may continue to be productive for about 50 years. Under cultivation, however, the plants are renewed every ten years. Propagation is by cuttings and the young plants are trained up stakes or sturdy trees with deep roots, which do not deprive the vanilla plant of nutrients. The tree's foliage also protects the vanilla plant from direct sunlight, thus replicating the conditions similar to those of the equatorial forests where wild vanilla grows.

Vanilla flowers (**above**) must be individually pollinated as soon as they open. Seven months later they will produce slender green pods (**right**). The harvested pods are steeped in hot water then laid out in the sun, under sheets. After being kept in a drier for a few weeks, the pods are packed into boxes. Their full aroma takes several months to develop.

Frosted vanilla

This is the most exquisitely flavoured of all types of vanilla. It is known as frosted vanilla as, after a long slow process, vanilla crystals form on the surface of the pod; these have the appearance of almost pure-white sparkling frost. Good-quality vanilla pods are black, flexible, plump and fleshy.

To produce this frosted effect, the pods are dried naturally in the sun, rather than artificially in an oven. They are not steeped in boiling water and no artificial preservatives are used.

In some countries, including Réunion, the freshly harvested pods are repeatedly steeped in water heated to 900°C. They are then rolled in sheets laid out in the sun so that they become soft. After being processed in a drier, they are stored in tin bins for several months, during which time they become covered in crystals and develop their full aroma.

A MEXICAN MONOPOLY

The Spanish discovered vanilla in Mexico, where it was used to flavour chocolate. Demand for vanilla in Europe did not begin until the 19th century. The monopoly over the cultivation of vanilla was long held by Mexico. This is because the vanilla plant's flowers are pollinated by an insect that exists only in Mexico. It was not until 1841, when Edmund Albius, a slave from Réunion, developed a method of artificial pollination, that the cultivation of vanilla spread to other tropical countries.

THE FINEST OF ALL SPICES

The distinctive flavour of vanilla is due to the high proportion of vanillin (a crystalline substance also found in fruit) in the pods. In Western cuisine vanilla is traditionally used in sweet dishes, such as cakes, creams, ice cream, chocolate, rice pudding, preserved fruit, pancake mixture, apple tart, and floating islands. In modern cuisine, however, it is increasingly used in savoury dishes. Vanilla keeps well in the glass vials in which it is often sold, or in glass jars. When buying vanilla, choose dark brown pods, which should be supple and covered in small white crystals. Vanilla pods without crystals are of an inferior quality.

The island of Madagascar is a major producer of vanilla. Malagasy vanilla is of a very high quality, the pods being long, narrow and very black. Every stage of the process, from the pollination of the flowers to the harvesting, sorting and drying of the pods, seen here at a plantation in northeastern Madagascar, is done by hand.

Opposite page: Although vanilla is usually used to flavour sweet dishes like this crème caramel, its subtle aroma lends it to all sorts of imaginative uses.

Spices in the garden

*Y*ou can grow certain spices in your own garden. Some, like love-in-a-mist, have acclimatized to cool climates and are easy to grow. Others, which are usually cultivated as vegetables, aromatic herbs and spice plants, are also decorative and can easily be incorporated into a flower bed. Fennel, saffron, dill, poppies and perhaps a small juniper tree will enhance an ornamental garden, adding a touch of delicacy and exoticism.

Dill

This spice, on which a tax was levied in biblical times, is mentioned in St Matthew's Gospel. The plant is an attractive aromatic herb, and its seeds have a flavour similar to fennel, to which it is closely related.

YELLOWISH-GREEN FLOWERS

Dill has delicate, umbrella-shaped flowers, which are an almost luminous yellowish-green. They are particularly attractive in a flower bed but as cut flowers they also make beautiful bouquets that perfume the air with their delicate fragrance. Dill gives an ethereal quality to flower arrangements because it has such tall stems, which can be over a metre (3 feet) long.

Dill, or *Aneth graveolens*, is indigenous to Asia and southern Europe. It grows in the arid, sun-baked soil and along country roadsides in the South of France, for example.

To grow in a garden, it needs plenty of warm sunshine but will tolerate poor soil. It should be sown out of doors in March or April and its seeds can be harvested in late summer, or a little earlier depending on the region.

A HINT OF MINT AND FENNEL

The dill plant is grown for its seeds, which are used to flavour fish and potatoes as well as jams and yogurts, and also liqueurs. Dill seeds can be used whole with fish, or ground and added to various recipes. Dill is also an aromatic herb; the leaves can be chopped into soups and salads.

A sprig of fresh dill, showing the plant's delicate stems and wispy leaves.

Salmon marinated in dill

Serves 6

6 salmon fillets, 150 g (5 oz) each, thinly sliced
30 grams of coarse salt
2 teaspoons of sugar
2 teaspoons of white peppercorns, coarsely ground
1 teaspoon of red peppercorns, coarsely ground
3 tablespoons of olive oil
a few dill seeds
20 sprigs of fresh dill

Arrange some of the dill sprigs at the bottom of a terrine. Mix the salt, sugar and pepper together and sprinkle a little of the mixture on to the dill. Then fill the terrine with alternating layers of salmon, some of the seasoning and a few sprigs of dill. Cover with foil and gently compress with a weight (such as a tin of food on top of a small slab of wood). Marinate for 24 hours in the refrigerator, turning the salmon from time to time. Remove the salmon slices from the terrine and wipe them clean. Arrange on a dish, drizzle with olive oil and decorate with fresh dill leaves.

Celery

Celery is a familiar plant in the vegetable garden. It is grown for its seeds, which are used as a spice, and for its succulent stems and aromatic leaves. It is related to celeriac but is quite distinct from this vegetable, which is grown for its large, globular root.

WILD ORIGINS

Wild celery, known as smallage, is an annual or biennial plant of the parsley family. Every part of the plant has a strong flavour and a slightly bitter taste. It grows along the edges of paths and tracks, particularly in moist places. Under cultivation, wild celery eventually became good to eat. *Apium graveolens*, var. *dulce*, is the familiar garden celery, which is as strongly flavoured as its wild cousin but has none of its bitterness.

The leaves are green or golden yellow and the stems are fleshy. Cultivated celery is instantly recognizable by its strong aroma and by the distinctive shape, colour and texture of its leaves and stem. There are several varieties of celery, each of a different size, flavour and colour, which is reflected in their names – such as Solid White, Greensnap and Giant Red. Celery is sown under cover in early spring, and is planted out in a sheltered position. The white umbrella-shaped flowerheads, which appear in summer, produce small, light brown seeds. These are harvested and used to flavour food.

Celery seeds are dark brown. Finely ground, they are mixed with salt, which they flavour and colour. A small amount of celery salt adds a delicious flavour to soups, eggs, vegetables, meat dishes and sauces. It can also be mixed into bread dough.

CELERY SEEDS

Celery seeds are brown, veined and very small. They can be used whole or ground to flavour salads, soups, raw vegetables, fried eggs and fish. They also add a good flavour to sauces and tomato juice.

In Scandinavia whole seeds are added to bread dough.

Used as an aromatic herb, celery leaves can be chopped into sauces or mixed into stuffings. The fleshy stems can be eaten raw, on their own or chopped into salads. The stems also make a delicious cooked vegetable, particularly when they are served with a cheese sauce. Celeriac, *Apium graveolens* var. *rapaceum*, which has a different taste, is grown for its large, plump root, which is grated and eaten either raw

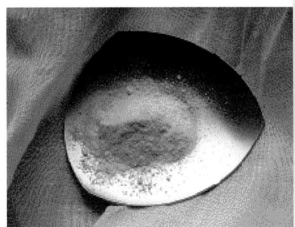

Both the leaves and the stem of the celery plant are used as aromatic herbs to flavour sauces and stuffings. Celery salt gives tomato juice a deliciously refreshing flavour but it also goes very well with many other fresh vegetable juices.

Flavoured salt

Salt is sometimes treated as a spice even though it does not come from a vegetable, as do all other spices.

White salt, including that from the Mediterranean, has been purified and is available as table salt or as coarse salt. Atlantic sea salt, which is grey, does not undergo a cleaning or purifying process so is a more natural salt. Fine sea salt, regarded as the best table salt, is very fine-grained and is very pure as it is gathered from salt pans.

All these different types of salt can be flavoured with herbs and spices. Celery salt, for example, is a mixture of salt and finely ground celery seeds. It is most often used to flavour tomato juice, and is a delicious addition to casseroles and salads, but can be added to almost any savoury dish.

Fennel

This tall, elegant member of the parsley family is indigenous to southern Europe, where it grows wild on sunny banks. Fennel is also easy to grow in the garden, either as a vegetable or as a herb. It also makes an attractive bedding plant.

ELEGANT AND AROMATIC

Common fennel, or *Foeniculum vulgare*, is a fine annual that can grow up to 1.50 m (5 feet) tall. The Romans knew it as *fenum*, the Latin word for hay, because of the hay-like aroma of its dried leaves. For use as a herb, fennel can be sown outdoors in summer, in well-drained soil and it must have a sunny position, otherwise the seeds do not ripen. The seedlings should be thinned, in order to bring on the strongest plants, which should be 60–90 cm (2–3 feet) apart. After the plant has flowered, and when the seeds are fully ripe, the heads can be cut and the seeds extracted by shaking the heads into a container. They must be left to dry, out of direct sunlight, for a few weeks and are then ready to be stored in jars or small plastic bags. Giant Bronze, a larger variety of fennel with brownish-purple leaves, is an ornamental plant that is often seen in English gardens. It has very delicate stems and feathery leaves, and produces a profuse growth of ethereal flowerheads.

Fennel has delicate, lace-like leaves. It has small, ridged seeds, which have a pervasive aniseed flavour. The taste is said to calm hunger pangs.

ANISEED FLAVOUR

Fennel seeds have a strong aniseed flavour. They are an ingredient of pastis and, dry-roasted or ground, they are used to flavour sauerkraut, sauces and mayonnaise, bread and cakes, liqueurs and many other sweet and savoury dishes.

A spice, a herb and a vegetable

Fennel has many uses. As a medicinal plant, it stimulates the appetite and aids digestion. It is also an aromatic herb, a spice and a vegetable. The variety of fennel that is eaten as a vegetable is Florence fennel, or *Foeniculum dulce.*
Florence fennel is easy to cultivate, and can be grown in the same way as common fennel. The bulbs are harvested in the autumn.

Both common fennel and the larger Giant Bronze make effective bedding plants, their diaphanous yellow flowers creating an impression of lightness and delicacy. Used by themselves or in combination with other flowers, fennel flowers are also very effective in flower arrangements.

Juniper

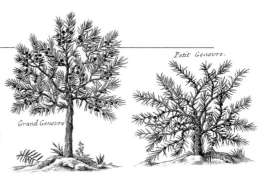

Grand Genevre.

Petit Genevre.

Juniper is a small shrublike conifer. In Europe it grows wild on downland and on the edges of woods, and is also widespread in Asia and North America. Juniper is grown for its aromatic berries but also makes an attractive garden shrub.

Originally prized for their medicinal virtues, juniper berries were later treated as a spice. Dried juniper berries are used to flavour autumn and winter dishes, such as game and sauerkraut.

TALL TREE, LOW-GROWING SHRUB

Juniperus communis is an attractive evergreen conifer. Bushy and hardy, it generally grows no taller than 3 metres (10 feet) in northern Europe, although in limestone areas it can reach a height of 10 metres (33 feet). At high altitudes or in peaty soil, by contrast, it grows as a low, ground-hugging shrub. The juniper has spiky, needle-like leaves, which are greyish-blue with a silvery sheen, and which cover the branches in a bushy, disorderly mass. The whole tree, from the berries to the bark, has an intense aroma.

PINE-FLAVOURED BERRIES

The juniper has very small white flowers, which are almost invisible on the tree. These mature into green berries very similar in size and shape to garden peas. The berries are ripe when they have turned a deep purple, and it is at this stage that they are harvested. After a long drying process, they become hard but retain a pungent, fiery pine flavour. Dried juniper berries are traditionally used to flavour sauerkraut but also go well with game, pâté and cabbage. They are also an ingredient of several northern European alcoholic drinks, such as gin, juniper liqueur and certain beers. In Scotland juniper berries are used in the production of smoked salmon.

Many small distilleries in northern Europe still use juniper berries to make gin and juniper liqueur or to flavour alcoholic drinks. Most of these distilleries, like Claeyssens in Wambrechies, northern France, still use traditional equipment.

Juniper liqueur

The Claeyssens distillery in northern France was established in 1817. Using traditional equipment and a historic grain mill, the distillery produces high-quality juniper liqueur.

For a single distillation the ingredients are 3 tonnes (2.95 tons) of rye, 1 tonne (0.98 ton) of malted barley, 4,000 litres (7,040 pints) of water, 40 kilos (88 lb) of yeast and just 2 kilos (4½ lb) of juniper berries. After two separate distillation processes, this volume of ingredients produces 3,000 litres (5,280 pints) of liqueur.

From top to bottom: Grinding machines; scales for weighing juniper berries; an alambic; tasting; the finished product packaged for sale.

Love-in-a-mist

With white and blue flowers enveloped in a delicate filigree of leaves, love-in-a-mist has an unusual appearance. The attractive pod is filled with small seeds. These can be used as a condiment and are also a mild stimulant, particularly for the appetite.

A DELICATE FLOWER

Love-in-a-mist, also known as fennelflower, is a small annual of the ranunculus family. Although it is indigenous to the Mediterranean basin, it can also be grown in more northern regions. Only *Nigella sativa*, the cultivated variety also known as black cumin, produces the seeds that are used as a spice. Wild love-in-a-mist grows in chalky soil and produces delicate light blue flowers.

The garden variety is *Nigella damascena*; Miss Jekyll Blue, which has larger flowers, is particularly popular. The seeds of *Nigella damascena* can also be used as a spice, but they have less flavour than those of *Nigella sativa*.

Love-in-a-mist can be sown in the garden in springtime, and it will flower the following summer. It prefers well-drained soil and a sheltered, sunny position.

The flower pod and seeds of *Nigella damascena*, the garden variety of love-in-a-mist. *Nigella sativa*, or black cumin, produces the tiny lemon-flavoured seeds that are used as a spice.

A HINT OF LEMON

The seeds of love-in-a-mist have a peppery flavour with
a hint of lemon. The seeds are one of the ingredients of Chinese
five-spice powder. The plant is also known as black cumin
because the seeds stimulate the appetite. To bring out their
flavour, it is best to toast the seeds before grinding them.
They can be used to flavour salads, ratatouille and boiled
potatoes. In Eastern cuisine they are added to bread and cakes.

Blue flowers

The plants in a herb or spice
garden can be arranged
according to the colour of their
flowers. To create a bed with
mixed shades of blue, or blues
that shade into one another,
combine love-in-a-mist with the
following:
- lavender, of which there are
  several types and varieties
- aquilegia (*Aquilegia vulgaris*),
  which has deep blue flowers
- anenomes (*Pulsatilla vulgaris*),
  whose bell-like flowers appear
  in early spring
- rosemary, an essential plant in
  a herb garden
- thyme, which produces
  cushions of purple flowers
- violets, with their sweet-
  smelling flowers, particularly
  those of *Viola odorata*
- sage (*Salvia officinalis*), which
  looks attractive all year round.

Love-in-a-mist's light-blue flowers go
well with other blue-flowered plants in
the herb garden, such as lavender,
thyme, rosemary and sage.

Designing your spice garden

*A*lthough spices are grown primarily for their culinary and medicinal uses, a spice garden offers the creative gardener great scope. Many herbs and spice plants come from the Mediterranean and, with their contrasting colours and textures, these sun-loving plants produce impressive displays.

A monastic tradition

The earliest herb gardens were those that were established by monks, who lovingly tended them within the confines of their monasteries. Occupying small patches of fertile soil and guarded from prying eyes by the high walls of monastic buildings, these gardens were traditionally laid out in neat square or rectangular beds, which also made it easier for the monks to tend the plants and harvest their precious seeds. The plants were grouped according to type: there were plants grown for use as spices and condiments, aromatic and medicinal plants, and plants grown to be used as dyes.

At that time, such plants were highly prized and the secrets of their various uses were jealously guarded.

The herb garden at the abbey of St Gallen, in Switzerland, is a good example for modern gardeners. Ancient documents show that it was laid out in geometric fashion, and that each bed was planted with just one species of plant.

A classic garden

The way you lay out your own spice garden depends on what you want to grow in it, how much space is available, and how much time you can spend tending it. Geographical location is another important consideration, as some Mediterranean plants may not survive in more a northerly climate without extra care. A very basic herb garden can consist of no more than a few herbs or spice plants growing just outside the kitchen door, or in pots placed on a terrace or veranda. If you have more space, a small herb garden can be made in a patch of ground in a corner of a flower or vegetable garden. The best way of all is to lay out a traditional spice garden enclosed within hedges or walls, which will give your plants the maximum shelter, with a box hedge backing each bed.

Herbs, spices and mixed borders

To create an informal garden, with contrasting clumps of texture and colour, you can fill your beds with a medley of herbs, spice plants and flowering plants. Many spice plants are also highly ornamental, and add a delicate touch to flowerbeds. Their flowers and foliage can be very beautiful, and you can still harvest their seeds at the appropriate time of year, and store them in jars for use in the kitchen. You can also intersperse your spice plants with such culinary herbs as thyme, basil, mint, tarragon, parsley, sage and rosemary. To show them to best advantage, you can arrange them either by flavour and aroma – with lemon-scented verbena and minty pelargonium for flavouring ice-cream mixtures, creams and syrups, for example – or in such a way that they create contrasts with the size and shape of their leaves and the colour of their flowers. Plants grouped according to the colour of their flowers, such as pinks and blues, also make impressive displays. Since many herb and spice plants are evergreen, you will also be able to enjoy your garden in the depths of winter.

Poppy

Poppies have large red, white or purple flowers and their tiny mauvish-black seeds have an almond-like flavour. The poppy is also a medicinal plant, whose seeds are used as a cure for many illnesses, but its seed capsules contain opium, a noxious substance.

Top right:
The delicate almond-like flavour of poppy seeds complements both sweet and savoury food, like this onion roll, a Polish speciality.

Right:
A bud, open flower and seed case of *Papaver somniferum*, whose seed capsules produce opium.

SIMPLICITY ITSELF

Poppies are so attractive and so easy to grow in the garden that their value as a spice and as the source of opium, a powerful narcotic, is sometimes hard to believe. The plant is an annual, and exists there are several varieties, including the corn poppy. The seeds are planted *in situ* in spring and plants flower the following summer. It is also self-seeding and can establish itself in the most unexpected places. Poppies growing in a field of ripe corn or barley are one of the most picturesque sights of the countryside in summer, but farmers regard the poppy as an unwelcome invader.

Although the poppy is indigenous to Greece and the East, it is very hardy and can survive in cool climates. When it is in flower, it reaches a height of 50–70 cm (20–28 inches). Its grey-green leaves provide a perfect foil for the flowers, which may be red, purple or purplish-pink with a black spot at the base of each petal. The flowers produce capsules that contain tiny purplish-black seeds. When the capsules are completely ripe, they can be slit in order to release the seeds.

SEEDS AND OIL

Poppy seeds have a delicate almond-like flavour. Dried, dry-roasted or ground, they can be sprinkled on green salads, fruit salads and creams. They can also be added to cake mixture. Poppy-seed oil is excellent for salad dressings and can also be used in cooking. It is not, however, widely available in delicatessens but should be found in specialist food shops. The best-quality poppy-seed oils come from the first, cold pressing of the seeds.

The poppy's seed capsules are attractive in bouquets of fresh flowers and in dried flower arrangements. The capsules contain small black seeds which can be extracted by slitting the capsule when it is fully matured and quite dry.

Main varieties

There are many varieties of poppy, some of which are purely ornamental. One of the best known is the corn poppy, which can take root in almost any ground.

The opium poppy, *Papaver somniferum*, is the source of analgesic and sedative drugs for the pharmaceutical industry and the variety from which the narcotic drug opium is extracted. There are several species of opium poppy, some with single flowers, some with double, and others with fringed petals. Commercial cultivation of the opium poppy is illegal.

The bright red corn poppy, *Papaver rhoeas*, is a wild variety, but garden varieties also exist. Like the opium poppy, its seeds are edible and can be used as a spice.

The Iceland poppy, *Papaver nudicaule*, has white, bright yellow or orange flowers.

Papaver orientale has orange, scarlet, white or salmon-pink flowers. There are many garden varieties.

Saffron

Already grown throughout Europe at the time of Alexander the Great, saffron is the most highly prized of spices, and it is even more costly than vanilla or cardamom. This is probably because, even today, it can only be harvested by hand.

THE GOLDEN CROCUS

Saffron, *Crocus sativus*, is an autumn-flowering crocus with long, thin leaves, purple flowers and large, bright orange stigmas. It should not be confused with the autumn crocus or meadow saffron, *Colchicum autumnale*, which is poisonous and which belongs to the lily family, although it has crocus-like flowers. The saffron crocus is grown for its stigmas, which are almost literally worth their weight in gold as they can only be harvested by hand, and which are used not only to flavour and colour food but also as a dye. For thousands of year, saffron was indeed used primarily as a dye; the Greeks and the Romans used it to turn textiles, woollen cloth and floor coverings a bright golden yellow.

SAFFRON IN THE GARDEN

Under cultivation, saffron bulbs are planted in summer. They flower from mid-September to mid-October, and it is in this four-week period that their stigmas are harvested. The leaves appear after the plant has flowered. Each bulb flowers only once but, soon after flowering, it develops bulbils (new, small bulbs), which will produce flowers years later.

Le Safran

"Le meilleur, le mieux nourri, et le plus estimé safran, est celuy de Boisne en Gatinois, où il est cultivé avec grand soin, étant presque toute la richesse du pays..."

"Des Drogues" Livre VI XVIIIᵉ siècle

Boynes, in the Gâtinais region of southwestern France, was the international capital of saffron from the 16th to the 19th centuries. Plate in the Maison du Safran in Boynes (**left**) inscribed with an 18th-century text, which reads: 'The finest, most luxuriant and most highly prized saffron comes from Boisne in Gatinois, where it is diligently cultivated, as it is the region's greatest wealth.'

Crocus grows best in well-drained, sandy soil in a sunny position. Indigenous to Greece or Italy, it is best suited to a Mediterranean climate. However, as it can survive temperatures of minus 15°C, it can be grown in northern Europe, but is sensitive to excessively cold, wet conditions. Extensive saffron plantations were established in Britain in the 16th century and continued to thrive into the 1700s. In France saffron has been grown in southern and central France, particularly in the Avignon region and in the Gâtinais. Although particularly cold winters may pose a threat, it is quite possible to grow saffron in the garden, not only for its beautiful flowers but also for its stigmas.

Safrant

Safrant Bâtard

Left:
Saffron is a variety of crocus that is easy to grow in the garden purely for its beautiful purple flowers. An 18th-century engraving of saffron and of a variety of marigold known as false saffron, since this flower's dried petals were used as a cheaper substitute for genuine ground saffron.

Above:
Saffron is usually sold in plastic sachets, either ready ground or in the form of whole dried filaments, but can also be bought loose, by the gram or pound. Saffron is very expensive, and dried marigold petals are sometimes dishonestly offered to buyers instead.

Above and below: Miniature tableaux in the Maison du Safran in Boynes, France, showing how saffron was once harvested, weighed and sifted.

To obtain a useable amount of saffron, saffron bulbs should be planted in a single patch, in August. Prepare an area of ground measuring about 2 m² (2.4 sq yd) and choose about 100 bulbs, which should not be smaller than 20 mm (0.8 in) across. Plant the bulbs at intervals of 12 cm (4.7 in), in rows 20 cm (7.9 in) apart. In October, these bulbs should produce at least 100 flowers, although these will yield just 1 gram (0.04 oz) of dried saffron. Leave the bulbs in the ground for another year. That October you should have enough flowers to produce three or four times as much dried saffron as the first year. In June after this second flowering, dig up all the bulbs, which will have produced bulbils (new, smaller bulbs). Lay them out to dry in the air, out of

direct sunlight, for two or three days. Pick them over, removing the loose papery outer skin but leaving enough to cover them, and store in a dark, dry place. In August, pick out the largest bulbs and replant them. You should have about four times as many bulbs as you started with two years ago. Plant the smaller bulbils in a nursery – closer together and shallower – to bring them on.

Left:
A bolting-machine, in which saffron is sifted.

Below:
Early 20th-century labels from the packaging of saffron grown in France.

Right:
An antique
saffron box.

From the fourth
year, your saffron
patch should
produce about
10 g (0.4 oz) of
saffron, more
than enough for a
year's supply.
To harvest the
stigmas, carefully
pull them from
the flowers and

spread them out in a sieve to dry, exposing them to gentle heat –
for example, near an open fire but not so close to the hearth
that they are tainted by the smell of smoke.

FLAVOUR AND COLOUR

Saffron has a strong and long-lasting flavour. It is used to
colour and flavour rice, it imparts a delicious aroma to sauces
that go well with fish, and it can be added to soups and
vegetables. Saffron also gives Spanish *paella* its distinctive
colour, and is used in French *bouillabaisse* and *rouille*,
a mayonnaise with garlic and chilli peppers.
Certain liqueurs, including chartreuse, owe
their mellow colour to saffron.

Saffron from the Gâtinais

Saffron was first cultivated in the Gâtinais region of France after the Crusades. Cultivation reached its peak in the 16th and 17th centuries By the late 1940s, these saffron plantations had dwindled. Not only had several harsh winters decimated the bulb fields, but the industry was also hit by rising labour costs and lessening demand. However, thanks to a small number of growers, saffron cultivation was revived, and since the late 20th century saffron plantations are once again productive.

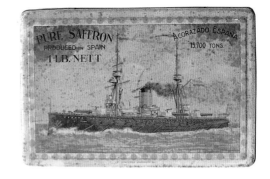

Opposite page and right:
A collection of boxes in which saffron grown in Britain and France was once packaged for export.

Aromatic spices

*F*or thousands of years, not only the flowers, leaves, fruit and seeds of certain plants but also their roots, wood, bark, gum and resin have been used in the preparation of perfumes. But, as Pliny the Elder observed in the first century AD, the fragrance of a perfume is appreciated by others but wasted on the wearer, who becomes unaware of it. Many perfumes contain spices, which can give the most captivating fragrances a magical warmth or a touch of Eastern mystery.

Florine Asch

Spices used in perfumes

Perfumes have been used since ancient times, and in almost all the great early civilizations, including those of Ancient Egypt, Greece and Rome. Over the centuries, the ingredients of perfumes have hardly changed, although perfumers continue to guard the secrets of their mixtures. Among the key ingredients of perfumes are spices, which come from any part of a plant, from the bark to the root.

Jean-François Laporte, who makes new perfumes by traditional methods, uses many spices in the creation of his fragrances. He believes that they give woody and flowery fragrances a unique sparkle, brilliance and excitement.

FLOWER BUDS

Mixed with the scent of roses, cloves produce a delicious perfume reminiscent of the scent of carnations. This scent is a constituent of Guy Laroche's *Fidji* and of Ralph Lauren's *Polo*, a spicy, aromatic men's cologne, which also contains other spices, such as coriander and chilli. Saffron is also used in many perfumes.

ROOTS

Root ginger is often combined with the aroma of flowers and fruit, as in *Parfum de Peau* by Montana, a sophisticated perfume that also contains blackcurrant and narcissus.

BARK

Cinnamon, a spice deriving from the dried bark of the cinnamon tree, has a gentle warmth and a pervasive aroma. It is an ingredient of *Safari*, by Ralph Lauren, and it adds a touch of sensuality to this exotic yet warm fragrance.

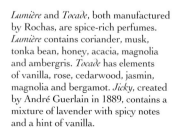

Lumière and *Tocade*, both manufactured by Rochas, are spice-rich perfumes. *Lumière* contains coriander, musk, tonka bean, honey, acacia, magnolia and ambergris. *Tocade* has elements of vanilla, rose, cedarwood, jasmin, magnolia and bergamot. *Jicky*, created by André Guerlain in 1889, contains a mixture of lavender with spicy notes and a hint of vanilla.

FRUIT

Star anise is an ingredient of perfumes with a fresh fragrance. Nutmeg and mace are used in men's colognes, particularly those with woody notes and a fresh, spicy dimension. Vanilla, which has a smooth, rounded scent, is also used as a fixative. Chilli, by contrast, is used very sparingly.

BERRIES

Juniper berries give woody notes that evoke the aroma of pine forests. They are just one ingredient of *Drakkar* by Guy Laroche, a men's cologne with a dynamic, invigorating and slightly bohemian character.

SEEDS

Several types of aromatic seeds are also used in perfumes. Cardamom seeds give a hint of fruit and coriander seeds have a peppery scent. One of several perfumes that contain coriander is *Obsession*, by Calvin Klein, a fragrance with an Oriental character, which also contains mandarin, vanilla, orange flowers, sandalwood and incense. Fenugreek seeds, fennel seeds and coriander seeds were used to make perfumes in ancient Greece. Pepper, with its pungent note, is an ingredient of many brands of men's colognes, while aniseed is more usually present in perfumes with a fresh fragrance.

Vanilla

Vanilla has a gentle, sweet, warm and pervasive fragrance that gives a perfume sweetness and depth. However, rather than natural vanilla, perfumers prefer to use vanillin, a synthetic vanilla fragrance, as it blends more effectively with the other ingredients of perfumes. Vanillin has a particularly smooth fragrance, and it is an ingredient of almost all perfumes made by Guerlain. Combined with contrasting aromas, it can produce fragrances with an aura of mystery and voluptuousness.

The apothecaries of the past were well aware of the therapeutic properties of spices. Pepper, cinnamon, dill, juniper berries and other spices, whose precise curative properties have been long forgotten, were all used as the ingredients of various medicinal preparations and they imbue these potions with their subtle fragrance.

Spices in classic perfumes

*A*particular perfume suits a particular type of skin and reflects the wearer's individuality. Different perfumes suit different occasions and different times of day, as well as the seasons of the year and changing fashions. Spices are important ingredients across the range of women's perfumes and men's colognes.

Men's fragrances

Certain colognes for men contain one or more spices. These may be sweet and understated or more robust and full-bodied according to whether the perfumer wants to create a serene, heady fragrance or a more invigorating blend. *Horizon* by Guy Laroche, a cologne with a serene fragrance, contains three spices – nutmeg, chilli and pepper. *Safari for Men*, by Ralph Lauren, contains cinnamon and cloves, and a mixture of aromatic herbs, including lavender and basil, which produce a dynamic fragrance. When he created *Égoïste* by Chanel the perfumier Jacques Polge wanted to create a spicy, woody fragrance with vanilla notes. Among other ingredients, he used coriander and vanillin, which produce a fragrance with a robust character. In many men's colognes, spices are combined with woody, dusky scents with hints of lavender, creating fragrances that embody strength and vigour.

Women's fragrances

Vanilla – or, strictly speaking, vanillin, its synthetic equivalent – is one of the principal components of fragrances for women. Almost all perfumes made by Guerlain, including *Shalimar* and *Jicky*, contain vanilla notes. *Shalimar*, one of Guerlain greatest perfumes, consists of oil of bergamot, rose, jasmine, iris, vanillin, cinnamon, tonka bean and opopanax. This great perfume has a powerful fragrance, which is voluptuous, sweet, warm, sensual and sometimes provocative. An Oriental masterpiece created by Jacques Guerlain in 1921, it is the vanilla-based scent *par excellence* and it will never date. *Jicky*, which has hints of lavender and spicy, dusky notes, could be described as a sharper, more dynamic variant of *Shalimar*.

Opium, by Yves Saint-Laurent, is a spicy fragrance with vanilla notes. It contains mandarin, jasmine, myrtle, lemon, oil of bergamot, patchouli and oak moss, vanilla, coriander and clove. Created in 1977, its appeal lies in its sensual, voluptuous and mysterious character. It can also be described as spicy, fruity and woody, with an Oriental character. Its distinctive character and panache come from the spices it contains.

Spices such as cinnamon, cloves and vanilla are among the ingredients of many perfumes. They impart vivacity and intensity.

Aromatic spices in the home

Perfumed candles and perfume-burners, or bunches of dried lavender slowly burning in the hearth are effective air-fresheners. They can be used to purify and scent the air anywhere in the home. You can also make your own fragrant sachets and pot-pourri. Aromatic spices are the key ingredient in all of these.

POT-POURRI AND OTHER AIR FRESHENERS

The literal meaning of the French term *pot-pourri* is 'rotten pot'. It refers to the practice of allowing fresh flower petals to rot down to a solid, fragrant mass. By the 18th century the term 'pot-pourri' had become the term designating a mixture of aromatic plants for perfuming the home. Traditional pot-pourri consisted of five types of ingredients: fragrant flowers and petals, aromatic wood, roots and bark; aromatic plants; spices; a fixative; and essential oils. In grand country houses one room was always kept exclusively for drying all these ingredients; a log fire was kept burning and the ingredients of pot-pourri, which were gathered in the gardens and grounds of the house or imported from abroad, were laid out to dry in the warm air.

MAKING A POT-POURRI

There are many different ways of making a pot-pourri. You can use dried ingredients bought in shops or ones that you find in the garden or in the countryside. The ingredients that you choose will depend on individual taste. A particular mixture can be put together according to colour, or according to the kind of fragrance you want to create, or both of these factors. Experimenting will help you find a mixture that appeals to you. Ingredients can also be seasonal, so that you can create a

Above:
This pierced metal ball, made by the perfumier Jean-François Laporte, is called *Safran*, meaning saffron in French. Like a pomander, it contains fragrant spices and orange flowers, and imparts a delicious fragrance to the air.

Left:
A fragrant,
spicy pot-
pourri
consisting of a
mixture of star
anise,
cinnamon and
different-
coloured
peppercorns.

**Following
pages:**
Apothecaries
and herbalists'
shops, their
wooden
counters
covered with
small,
intriguing
packets of
sweet-smelling
herbs and
spices, were
once as easy to
find as bakers'
or butchers'
shops. A rare
survivor from
the past is the
Herboristerie
de la Place de
Clichy, in
Paris, which
sells an
enormous
range of herbs
and spices in
traditional
surroundings.

summer or a winter pot-pourri. It might consist of a single type of flower – such as rose or lavender – or of several (perhaps a combination of wild and cultivated flowers). The other ingredients might include aromatic herbs – such as sage, thyme, mint or rosemary – pieces of fragrant bark, small pine cones, berries or seeds and spices. These, particularly cinnamon, allspice, juniper berries, cloves, vanilla and star anise, add a degree of pungency to a pot-pourri, and give a hint of Oriental exoticism.

Spices also go well with citrus fruits and with dried lemon, orange or bergamot zest. Vanilla is a good complement to cinnamon, lavender and vetiver.

Spices make very attractive autumn pot-pourri because their colours combine well with the colour of bark. For a winter pot-pourri they can be added to dried leaves or pine cones.

The French perfumer Jean-François Laporte uses spices in his pot-pourri,

Left:
Dried marigold petals, star anise, cloves, lichen and orange essence are the ingredients of this pot-pourri created by the perfumer Jean-François Laporte.

Right:
Certain spices can be used to make sweet-smelling sachets, which can also be used to keep insects away.

one of which he has named *Spice Medley*. He uses spices –
particularly pepper, nutmeg, mace, cloves, coriander and star
anise – to add pungency to his pot-pourri mixtures and as a
fixative for the other ingredients.

FRAGRANT SACHETS
Sheets, duvet covers and pillow cases stored in a linen press
or clothes hanging in a wardrobe can be perfumed with
colourful canvas or silk sachets containing a
mixture of flowers, herbs and spices. The
more spices you use, the more fragrant
the mixture will be. Fragrant
sachets are easy to sew and, if
you live in the country, make
ideal presents for house guests,
especially if you embroider their
initials on the material.

Moth-repellent bags

Plants and spices that
have insect-repellent
properties can be used to
make fragrant sachets
that will keep moths
away from clothes and
linen. For the bags,
choose a material that
is sufficiently tightly
woven to contain the
mixed flowers, herbs
and spices, but loose
enough to allow
their fragrance to
escape.
The best insect-repelling herbs
are lavender, rosemary, tansy
and mint. You can either buy
these ready-dried in a herbalist's
shop or pick them fresh from
your garden. Mix them together
and add a few cloves, pieces of
nutmeg and mace, some cinnamon sticks and any other
ingredient you choose. Add some
powdered orris (the fragrant
rhizome of the Florentine iris) as
a fixative and sew the mixture
into a bag. Tie it up with a
ribbon, which can be used to
hang the bag in a wardrobe.

Recipes and further information

*I*n the past, using spices to preserve food was an elaborate culinary skill. Prized for their pungent flavours, spices were used to preserve meat and to lessen the unpleasantly strong flavour of certain dishes. Today, spices are of course used primarily for their flavour and aroma. This section contains a selection of recipes that include spices. This is followed by a list of sources from which you can obtain spices and a selection of books for further reading.

Recipes

Mixed green salad

Choose several different kinds of lettuce for this mixed salad. Add a generous selection of fresh herbs, such as mint, tarragon, chives, parsley, fennel and basil. Sprinkle the lettuce and the herbs with anise and poppy seeds. Add olive oil and lemon juice, and season with salt and pepper.

Pumpkin soup
Serves 4
1 pumpkin
½ litre (1 pt) of milk
1 tablespoon of crème fraîche
2 teaspoons of curry powder
1 teaspoon of cinnamon

Peel the pumpkin and chop it into even-sized cubes. Place in a large pan with enough water to cover and simmer for 30 minutes. Warm the milk and add it to the pumpkin pieces, then add the crème fraîche and the spices. Stir so that all the ingredients are well mixed. Add salt and pepper to taste. Transfer to a warm tureen and serve.

Marinated eggs

Hard-boil the eggs and crack but do not remove the shells. Fill a pan with salted water and add herbs and spices, such as bay, pepper, mustard seeds, rosemary, cumin and cloves, and some red wine. Bring this mixture to the boil then leave to cool. Then add the eggs and leave them to marinate for one to two days. Lift out the eggs and remove the shells. Cut the eggs in half, either lengthwise or across, remove the yolks and fill the whites with a vinaigrette dressing or other sauce. Replace the yolks, rounded side up.

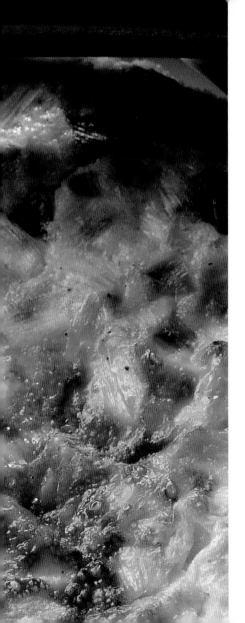

Leek tart with nutmeg

Serves 6

250 grams (9 oz) of shortcrust
pastry (pie crust)
600 grams (1 lb 5 oz) of leeks
200 grams (7 oz) of crème fraîche
60 grams (2 oz) of grated gruyère
3 eggs
50 grams (2 oz) of butter
6 pinches of freshly grated nutmeg
salt and pepper

Line a baking tin or ovenproof
dish with the pastry and bake it
blind. Wash and finely chop the
leeks. Melt the butter in a pan,
add the leeks and cook very
gently for 15 minutes. Break the
eggs into a bowl, beat, then add
the gruyère, nutmeg, salt,
pepper, and crème fraîche. Pour
this mixture into the pan with the
leeks and stir. Pour on to the
pastry and bake for 25 minutes at
200°C (400°F), Gas 6. Serve the
tart warm with a seasonal salad.

Monkfish with fresh ginger

Serves 6

1kg (2 lb) of monkfish fillets
a piece of root ginger about
7 cm (3 inches) long
the juice of 3 lemons
olive oil
salt and pepper

Poach the monkfish fillets in
salted water. Peel and finely
chop the ginger. Add it to the
lemon juice, together with the
olive oil, salt and pepper.
Arrange the monkfish on a
serving dish and pour over the
ginger dressing. Serve
with thinly sliced
leeks or with fresh
tagliatelle.

Sea bream à la Donostria

Serves 6
1 large sea bream
4 cloves of garlic, chopped
olive oil
4 tablespoons of vinegar
salt and pepper
1 Espelette pepper
(see page 59), finely chopped
juice of 1 lemon

Gut the fish and rinse in cold water. Drizzle it with olive oil and bake for 30 minutes at 200°C (400°F), Gas 6. Reserve the juices. Sprinkle the fish with salt and keep in a warm place.

Gently heat some olive oil in a pan then add the garlic and cook.
Pour the vinegar into a pan and boil to reduce it to half its volume. Add the lemon juice and the fish juices. Season with pepper and add the Espelette pepper. Pour this mixture into the pan with the fried garlic and simmer for 2 minutes.
Lay the monkfish on a serving dish and fill the cavity with the sauce. Serve with plain boiled rice or rice flavoured with spices.

Fish with ginger and cabbage

Serves 4
4 fish fillets of 150 g (5 oz) each
1 green cabbage
1 piece of fresh root ginger
a few juniper berries
crème fraîche

Blanch the cabbage by boiling it in salted water for 5 minutes Take off four large leaves. On each of them place a rolled-up fillet of fish, 2 or 3 juniper berries, a pinch of grated ginger and a teaspoon of crème fraîche. Drizzle with olive oil and season with salt and pepper. Wrap the fish in the cabbage leaf and secure with string, then steam for 20 minutes.

Pike perch with peppers and paprika

Serves 4

4 pike perch (ask your fishmonger to clean them)
3 plump red peppers
50 grams (2 oz) of paprika
2 or 3 star anise

Poach the fish in water for about 10 minutes, taking care not to overcook, as it will become too soft.

Cut the peppers in half, then remove and discard the seeds. Slice the paprika into thin strips and brown them in a little olive oil over a gentle heat for 10 minutes. Add the fish and quickly cook on both sides.

Remove the grains from the star anise pods and grind, reserving the pods. Arrange the fish on a serving dish, sprinkle them with the paprika and star anise and decorate with the pods of the star anise. Sorrel leaves lightly browned in a pan make an excellent accompaniment to this dish.

Curried rice

Serves 6
440 grams (14 oz)
of long-grain rice
3 medium onions, chopped
25 grams (1 oz) of curry powder
1 litre (2 pints) of stock
50 grams (2 oz) of butter

Melt the butter in a large pan and gently cook the onions until lightly browned. Add the rice and stir until transparent. Add the stock, season with salt and pepper and simmer for 10 to 15 minutes. Add the curry powder and simmer for a few more minutes, until the rice is cooked.

Vegetable rissoles

Serves 4
300 grams (10 oz) of split peas
2 onions, finely chopped
fennel seed
fresh coriander leaves
olive oil

Soak the split peas in water for about 12 hours. Drain and mill them. Place the crushed peas in a bowl and mix in the onions, fennel seeds and coriander leaves, and season with salt and pepper.
Shape the mixture into cakes and brown them on both sides in a pan in a little olive oil.

Vegetable samosas

Serves 4
mustard seeds
curry powder
2 onions
2 potatoes, peeled and cooked
50 grams (2 oz) of garden
peas, cooked
2 carrots, cooked
4 squares of filo pastry
olive oil

Chop and mix all the ingredients. Spoon a quarter of the mixture on to each of the pastry squares, then fold to make a triangle. Brown them on all sides in a pan in a little olive oil. Serve hot.

Crystallized ginger

500 grams (1 lb) of fresh ginger
3 tablespoons of water
500 grams (1 lb) of sugar

Thinly slice the ginger. Put it in a pan and gently simmer for about half an hour, until it is quite soft.

Remove the ginger and weigh it. Return it to the pan with an equal weight of sugar and 3 tablespoons of water. Cook over a gentle heat until it becomes dry. Then toss in sugar and leave to cool. Transfer to an airtight container. It will keep for up to three months.

Spiced pears

Serves 6
10 pears
2 bottles of red wine
1 clove
8 coriander seeds
8 peppercorns
1 cinnamon stick
100 grams (4 oz) of fresh ginger
1 vanilla pod
350 grams (12 oz) of sugar
orange zest

Pour the wine into a pan and add all the spices, the sugar and the orange zest. Bring to the boil and simmer for 10 minutes. Peel the pears, add to the wine and let them simmer for 10 minutes. Lift them out and place in a large bowl. Boil the wine hard until it has reduced by half. Strain the liquid, which should have the consistency of syrup, and pour over the pears. Leave to cool, then refrigerate for 24 hours.

Bear's cake with cinnamon and cardamom

Serves 6
3 eggs
2 tablespoons of sugar
2 tablespoons of flour
1 tablespoon of whipping cream (or milk)
2 teaspoons of baking powder
2 teaspoons of ground cinnamon
1 teaspoon of whole cardamom seeds
1 teaspoon of ground ginger
2 cloves
1 teaspoon of freshly ground cardamom seeds
120 grams (4 oz) of margarine, melted

Preheat the oven to 170–200°C (340–390°F), Gas Mark 5–6 and grease a baking tin. Beat the eggs and sugar together until they have the consistency of thick, smooth cream. Mix together the flour, the baking powder and the spices and fold them into the mixture.

Stir in the milk, adding small amounts at a time, then stir in the margarine. Pour the mixture into the baking tin and bake for 45 minutes on the bottom shelf of the oven.

Chocolate mousse with ginger

Serves 4
440 grams (14 oz) of bitter chocolate
30 grams (1 oz) of preserved ginger, finely diced
a knob of butter
4 eggs
2 tablespoons of caster sugar
1 tablespoon of rum

Put the chocolate and the butter in a double boiler and melt over a gentle heat. Take the pan off the heat as soon as the chocolate has softened. Separate the eggs, adding the yolks to the chocolate in the double boiler. Add the rum and the ginger. Whip the egg whites until they form peaks, fold them into the mixture and leave to cool.

Cinnamon couscous

Serves 8 to 10
1 kg (2lb) of coarse semolina
150 (5 oz) grams of butter
water
salt
ground cinnamon
icing sugar
almonds, blanched

In this recipe the semolina is cooked in three stages. Pour the semolina into a dish, and add the salt and half a cup of water. Transfer it to a pan and steam it for 30 minutes. Pour it back into the dish and add 50 grams (2 oz) of butter. Leave to cool, then pour over 3 cups of water. Set aside to rest.
Repeat this process, reducing the cooking time to 15 minutes. Then steam the mixture a third time, for 20 to 25 minutes. Pour the mixture into a shallow dish, add 50 grams (2 oz) of butter and dust it with ground cinnamon, icing sugar and almonds.

Cinnamon biscuits

Makes 8 to 10 biscuits
250 (9 oz) grams of flour
125 grams (4 oz) of sugar
125 grams (4 oz) of almonds,
blanched
125 grams (4 oz) of butter
30 grams (1 oz) of ground
cinnamon
1 egg yolk, beaten

Chop the almonds and mix them with all the other ingredients. Lightly cover and leave for about 12 hours so that the flavours blend. Roll out the mixture and cut into shapes. Glaze each one by painting it with the egg yolk. Bake in a hot oven for 30 minutes.

Gingerbread

Serves 4 to 6
250 grams (9 oz) of flour
1 tablespoon of baking powder
a pinch of salt
2 cups of milk
50 grams of soft brown sugar
3 tablespoons of dark honey
30 grams (1 oz) of butter
3 tablespoons of mixed spices:
crushed aniseed, cinnamon,
cloves, nutmeg, cardamom and
ground star anise

Preheat the oven to 170°C (325°F), Gas 3 and grease a baking tin. Warm the milk in a pan, slowly stirring in the sugar and the honey. In a mixing bowl blend the flour, salt and spices.

When the milk is lukewarm, slowly stir it into the flour. Mix thoroughly, stirring with a wooden spoon for about 10 minutes. Pour the mixture into the baking tin and bake for about 1 hour.

Cherry jam with cinnamon

Makes 4 to 6 jars of jam
1 kg (2 lb) of eating cherries
1 kg (2 lb) of cooking cherries
1 kg (2 lb) of granulated sugar
50 grams (2 oz) of ground cinnamon

Wash and drain the cherries and pick off the stalks. Remove the stones, reserving a few to tie in a piece of muslin. Put the cherries, the sugar and the muslin in a mixing bowl.

Leave the mixture to macerate in a cool place for at least 3 hours, then drain, reserving the liquid. In a large pan, ideally a copper jam pan, bring the liquid to the boil and simmer for 10 minutes. Then add the cherries and the muslin.

When the cherries come to the boil, add the ground cinnamon and simmer for a further 10 minutes. Test the jam by placing a few drops on a cold plate. If they cool to a jelly, the jam is ready to be poured into sterilized jars.

Following this basic recipe, cinnamon can be used to flavour many other kinds of jams.

Makowiec

Serves 4 to 6

500 grams (1 lb) of poppy seeds
200 grams (7 oz) of icing sugar
2 egg whites
50 grams (2 oz) of butter
almond essence
zest of 1 lemon, grated
1 vanilla pod
30 grams (1–2 oz) of raisins
3 spoonfuls of honey

Makowiec is a Polish poppy-seed cake. Rinse the poppy seeds and place in a bowl. Cover them with boiling water to soften them. Strain through a tea towel and pulverize in a blender. Melt the butter in a pan and add the lemon zest, almond essence, raisins and honey. Stir the mixture over a gentle heat for 10 minutes.

Beat the egg whites until stiff, fold them into the mixture and set aside. Make a bread dough or brioche-style dough (cooking time will vary). Cover the dough or pastry with the mixture, roll it up and bake in the oven. When cooked, allow the cake to cool then cover it with icing made with 200 grams (7 oz) of sugar, the juice of a lemon, a tablespoon of water and a tablespoon of rum.

Fruit salad with cardamom

Serves 6

4 oranges, 1 apple
2 bananas, 1 pear
red currants, blackcurrants,
raspberries or other red fruit
fresh mint leaves
1 teaspoon of cardamom seeds
2 tablespoons of sugar
2 tablespoons of rum

Squeeze the juice from one of the oranges. Peel and cut the other oranges and the apple, bananas and pear into small pieces and put them in a large bowl with the red currants, blackcurrants and raspberries.

Pour the sugar, the rum and half a cup of water into a pan and gently heat until the sugar has dissolved. Then add the orange juice and the cardamom seeds. Pour this syrup over the fruit and decorate with mint leaves. Serve chilled.

Spiced herbal tea

Serves 1
**1 pinch of verbena, lemon balm or
lime blossom
2 cloves
2 cinnamon sticks
zest of 1 orange
sugar**

Put the spices and the orange
zest in a piece of muslin and tie
it up with string. Make a cup or
pot of herbal tea and add the
muslin bag, leaving it to draw
for at least 3 minutes. Drink
the tea while it is still hot, with
added sugar to taste.

Hot toddy

Serves 1
**1 pinch of tea
1 tablespoon of whisky or rum
3 cloves
1 cinnamon stick
sugar or runny honey**

Mix all the ingredients together.
Put them in a pan with a little
water and gently heat for 3
minutes. Pour into a cup, add
sugar or honey to taste, and
drink immediately.

Spiced tea

Serves 1
**1 pinch of Indian tea
2 cloves
1 cinnamon stick
3 cardamom pods
sugar**

Put all the ingredients in a pan
with a little water and simmer for
5 minutes.
Strain the liquid into a cup and
sweeten to taste.

Where to buy spices

Most large supermarkets offer a wide range of fresh and dried spices. Health-food stores are also a good source of spices, but these are more likely to be in dried form. The best places to find some of the more exotic spices, and spice mixtures in particular, are shops specializing in West Indian, Indian and Chinese food. Many specialist retailers, who can be contacted via the internet, stock a vast range of spices and provide a mail-order or direct delivery service.

Buying online in the UK

The Cool Chile Co
www.coolchile.co.uk
Website of The Cool Chile Co, specialists in dried chillies from Mexico, plus powdered mixtures and other condiments.

www.hardtofindfoods.co.uk
Website of Hard to Find Foods, offering all kinds of specialist foods, including herbs and spices.

www.simplyspice.co.uk
Indian food and spices.

www.GlobalSpices.co.uk
Herbs and spices from around the world.

www.seasonedpioneers.com
Spices, seasonings and chillies.

Buying online in the US

www.americanspice.com
Website of The Great American Spice Company. Offers spices and herbs, condiments and sauces.

www.theepicentre.com/spices
Asian, Indian, Mediterranean and Mexican collections of spices.

www.culinarycafe.com
Comprehensive links to online suppliers.

To visit

Museum in Docklands,
No. 1 Warehouse,
West India Quay,
Hertsmere Road,
London
E14 1AL
Tel. 0870 444 3857
www.museumindocklands.org
.uk
Contains a section devoted to mercantile activity in the port of London in the 16th, 17th and 18th centuries, when demand for spices in Britain was at its height. Open 10am–6pm daily.

Further reading

Phillippa Cheifitz, *Cooking with Chillies, Peppers & Spices*. New Holland, London, 1994.

Andrew Dalby, *Dangerous Tastes: The Story of Spices*. University of California Press, 2002.

Elizabeth David, *Spices, Salt and Aromatics in the English Kitchen*. Penguin, Harmondsworth, 1970.

Sarah Garland, *The Complete Book of Herbs & Spices. An Illustrated Guide to Growing and Using Culinary, Aromatic, Cosmetic and Medicinal Plants*. Frances Lincoln, London, 1979.

Carolyn Heal and Michael Allsop, *Cooking with Spices*. David & Charles, Vermont, 1983.

Tony Hill, *Contemporary Encyclopedia of Herbs and Spices: Seasoning for a Global Kitchen*. Wiley, London, 2004.

Madhur Jaffrey, *From Curries to Kebabs: Recipes from the Indian Spice Trail*. Crown, 2003.

Elizabeth Lemoine, *Spices*. Book Sales, 2002.

John Lust, *The Herb Book*. Bantam, New York, 1984.

Giles Milton, *Nathaniel's Nutmeg: or the True and Incredible Adventures of the Spice Trader who Changed the Course of History*. Penguin, London, 2000.

Sallie Morris, *A Culinary Guide to Choosing and Using Spices*. Anness, London, 2002.

Sallie Morris and Lesley Mackley, *The Cook's Encyclopedia of Spices*. Anness, London, 2003.

Jill Norman, *Herbs and Spices: The Cook's Reference*. Dorling Kindersley, London, 2002.

Jill Norman, *The Complete Book of Spices: A Practical Guide to Spices and Aromatic Herbs*. Studio Books, London, 1990.

F. Rosegarten Jr, *The Book of Spices*. Livingston, Philadelphia, 1969.

Wolfgang Schivelbusch, *Tastes of Paradise: A Social History of Spices, Stimulants and Intoxicants*. Vintage Books, 1993.

Malcom Stuart, *The Encyclopedia of Herbs and Herbalism*. Macdonald & Co., Turin, 1987.

Jack Turner, *Spice: The History of Temptation*. Knopf, New York, 2004.

Andre Vladimirescu, *The Spice Book*. Wiley, 1994.

Websites

www.AmericanSpice.com

Website of The Great American Spice Company. Information on spices and books.

www.astaspice.org

Website of the American Trade Association. Includes comprehensive information on the history of spices.

www.theepicentre.com/Spices

Encyclopedia of spices.

www.culinarycafe.com/ Spices_Herbs/index.html

Comprehensive section on spices, including a spice encyclopedia, recipes, and books on spices.

Acknowledgements

Marie-Françoise Valéry would like to thank Editions du Chêne, the publishers of the original French edition of this book, for having asked her to write on this fascinating subject. She also extends her thanks to Sophie Boussahba for having fired her enthusiasm with so many fine photographs, and to Jean-François Laporte, who generously provided her with information regarding the use of spices in the creation of perfumes.

Sophie Boussahba would like to thank all those individuals and institutions that assisted her in the preparation of this book:

Pierre Aragon, Opalix
Roberto Banfi
Barbara Bourgois
Christiane Boussahba
Michel Bouvot
Christophe Chalier
Henry Coste
Isabelle Martineau
Jean-Pierre Naivin
Catherine Nothias
Beata Malmquist
Patrice Pascal
Francis Pénaud
Misha and Potestad
Nicole and Ata Saudi

Christian Sindou
Véronique Vaude
Christian Vrillaud
Bibliotheque de l'Ordre des Pharmaciens, particularly Madame Kassel, keeper of the collections relating to the history of pharmacy
Guerlain
Chez Izraël, Paris
Plastiques
Rochas
Distillerie Claeyssens, Wambrechies, particularly M. Pley
Claire, the Indian spice shop
Kodak Professionel
Musée du Safran, Boynes
The press offices of Ricard and Pernod
Studio Elle

Photographic credits

All the photographs are by **Sophie Boussahba**, except for the following:
– Hachette-Livre picture library: pages 4, 17ab, 18, 19ab, 25a, 29b, 30a, 44ab;
– Ordre National des Pharmaciens, Collection d'histoire de la pharmacie: pages13a, 21a, 25b, 26b, 31b, 38a, 42a, 50b, 66b, 78c, 87b;
– Bios: pages 11 (Montford), 21b (Daniel Heulin), 22a (Michel Lefèvre), 22b (Julien Frébet), 34 (Edward/Still), 46–47(Julien Frébet), 48a (Monford), 67a and 69abc (Dominique Haleux), 82 (John Miller/Garden Picture Library);
– Jean Bras: page 16a, 26a, 59b, 63ab;
– Aziz Goulamaly: page 66a;
– Catherine Nothias: page 60b.

Production: Archipel Concept – Grignan
Graphic design: Editions du Chêne
Editor: Thomas Brisebarre, assisted by Rose-Hélène Lempereur
Layout: Thomas Brisebarre
Editorial director: J.-J. Brisebarre

First published by Editions du Chêne, an imprint of Hachette-Livre
43 Quai de Grenelle, Paris 75905, Cedex 15, France
Under the title *Les Epices*
© 1998, Editions du Chêne–Hachette Livre

English language translation produced by Translate-A-Book, Oxford
This edition published by Hachette Illustrated UK, Octopus Publishing Group
2–4 Heron Quays, London, E14 4JP
English translation © 2005, Octopus Publishing Group Ltd., London

ISBN 10: 1 84430 153 2
ISBN 13: 978 1 84430 153 9

Printed by Toppan Printing Co., (HK) Ltd.